S0-CFB-725

Kestrel skeleton

White-bellied
sea eagle

Verreaux's eagle

European kestrel

EYEWITNESS BOOKS

EAGLE

Common, or
crested, caracara

& BIRDS OF PREY

Written by
JEMIMA PARRY-JONES
The National Birds of Prey Centre, England

Photographed by
FRANK GREENAWAY

Saker falcon

Bald eagle

ALFRED A. KNOPF • NEW YORK

African hawk eagle

Peregrine falcon

Egyptian vulture

Foot of wedge-tailed eagle

White-backed vulture

African harrier hawk

DK

A DORLING KINDERSLEY BOOK

Project editor David Pickering
Art editor Kati Poynor
Assistant editor Julie Ferris
Managing editor Gill Denton
Managing art editor Julia Harris
Production Charlotte Traill
Picture research Rachel Leach
DTP designer Nicola Studdart
Consultant Colin Shawyer

This is a Borzoi Book published by Alfred A. Knopf, Inc.

This Eyewitness® Book has been conceived by Dorling Kindersley Limited and Editions Gallimard

First American edition, 1997
Copyright © 1997 by Dorling Kindersley Limited, London.
All rights reserved under International and Pan-American Copyright Conventions. Published in the United States of America by Alfred A. Knopf, Inc., New York. Distributed by Random House, Inc., New York. Published as *Eyewitness: Eagle* in Great Britain by Dorling Kindersley Limited, London, in 1997.

"Eyewitness" is a trademark of Dorling Kindersley Limited and is used by Alfred A. Knopf, Inc., under license.

http://www.randomhouse.com/

Printed in Singapore
0 9 8 7 6 5 4 3 2 1

Library of Congress Cataloging-in-Publication Data
Parry-Jones, Jemima.
Eagle: & birds of prey/written by Jemima Parry Jones;
photographed by Frank Greenaway.
p. cm. — (Eyewitness Books)
Includes index.
Summary: Describes the anatomy, hunting techniques, mating, nesting, and eating habits of birds of prey.
1. Birds of prey—Juvenile literature.
[1. Birds of prey.] I. Title. II. Series
QL696.F3P386   1997
598.9'1—dc20   96-36420
ISBN 0-679-88543-9 (trade)
ISBN 0-679-98543-3 (lib. bdg.)

Color reproduction by
Colourscan, Singapore
Printed in Singapore by Toppan

Contents

Tawny eagle

What is a bird of prey?

BIRDS OF PREY are not the only birds that hunt for their food, nor the only birds that eat meat, or have hooked beaks, or fly very well, but they are the only birds that combine all these characteristics, and with them, one very distinctive feature: They kill with their feet. They are called raptors, from the Latin *raptare*, to seize or grasp, because they seize their prey in their feet. Their lethal talons can snatch fish from the water, strike birds out of the air, and rip open animal quarry (prey). Like lions and tigers, raptors are "top predators": They hunt other creatures, but nothing hunts them, except for other raptors – and humans.

SPECIAL DIET
Some raptors will eat just about anything; others are specialists. One of the most specialized is the snail kite of Florida. It lives on a diet of water snails. Its beak has a long, curved hook with which to remove the snail from its shell.

Primary feathers, like tail feathers, are fanned out for landing

Tail is used for steering, soaring, and braking

Large vultures have powerful beaks, to rip open the carcasses of large animals

The feet of vultures, such as these white-backed vultures, are weak because they don't need to kill their prey

CATCH IT WHEN IT'S DEAD
There is a major exception to the rule that birds of prey hunt their food: vultures. Vultures are specialized in scavenging, that is, finding dead animals, rather than hunting live ones. Other raptors will eat carrion (dead flesh) if they happen to come across it, but only vultures are carrion specialists. Most vultures spend much of their time soaring high in the sky, scanning a wide area for signs of death.

8

SYMBOL AND STANDARD
Many peoples have taken birds of prey as symbols of what they most revere: gods, freedom, the sun, royalty. Many nations, kings, and armies have taken birds of prey as their emblems. This eagle standard comes from the French army, c.1800.

Ravens eat meat in much the same way as many birds of prey

CARNIVOROUS BIRDS
Many meat-eating birds are not birds of prey. For example, magpies hunt and kill small birds. Ravens such as these, which belong to the crow family, have a diet similar to that of buzzards. They have strong, pointed beaks with which they kill young rabbits and even the occasional lamb. But only raptors kill with their feet.

Wing feathers fan out to give extra lift (pp. 16–17)

BORN TO KILL
Birds of prey are perfect hunters. The tawny eagle pictured here is a superb flier, and has the characteristic lethal raptor feet. Its curved beak and claws act as a knife and fork for tearing through flesh to eat the prey. Raptors' skill as hunters can work against them if the environment becomes polluted: If each animal they eat contains a tiny amount of pollutant, they end up taking in a large amount. So environmental damage often hurts them first.

Female merlins are usually one-third heavier than males; this is average for falcons

In some birds of prey, the male is much more colorful than the female

DOES SIZE MATTER?
Birds of prey are unusual in that the females are usually bigger than the males. (Scientists call this "reverse sexual dimorphism.") The size difference varies. It is greatest in sparrowhawks, where the female is twice the size of the male. Vultures are one of the exceptions: Males and females are usually the same size, and male condors are larger than female condors.

Killing feet: Powerful with huge, curved talons for grasping prey

The raptor families

THERE ARE RAPTORS on every continent except Antarctica: Over 300 species of diurnal (day-flying) birds of prey, and about 130 owl species. Each of these species plays its own unique part in the ecosystem. Scientists class all the day-flying birds of prey together in the "order" (group) Falconiformes, which contains five separate "families." The owls have their own order, the Strigiformes. Scientists give each order, family, and species a Latin name. The local names for each bird change with language and region, but the Latin name is always the same so that scientists and others do not become confused. The Latin names of the birds in this book can be found in the index on p. 60.

Black vulture flying; vultures soar to look for dead animals

The powerful king vulture; New World vultures, like storks, urinate on their own legs to keep cool

OSPREY
Ospreys form a one-species family: They are unique and cannot be classed with any others. Specialists at catching fish (the only raptors that dive deeply into the water), they eat very little else. They are "cosmopolitan," that is, found worldwide, where there is shallow water – lakes, rivers, or coastal areas.

Pandionidae
osprey

osprey

Bengal eagle owl flying

Spectacled owl, so called because of its facial markings

Iranian eagle owl chicks

NEW WORLD VULTURES
These vultures live in the Americas. They occupy the niche in the food chain that the Old World vultures fill in the rest of the world: eating up carrion. Although they look quite similar to other vultures, they are, in fact, more closely related to storks than to any other raptors and so, according to recent scientific research, should no longer be classed in the Falconiformes order. There are seven species of New World vulture.

Andean condor, largest of all raptors

SECRETARY BIRD
Secretary birds, found in Africa, are another unique species, in a family of their own. They have much longer legs than other raptors, stand 1.2 m (4 ft) tall, and hunt by walking, not flying, across grasslands, and stamping on the prey they find.

Sagittariidae
secretary bird

secretary bird

OWLS – RAPTORS OF THE NIGHT
Owls are not related to the diurnal birds of prey. Most are nocturnal (hunt at night) or crepuscular (hunt at dawn and dusk). Their sight is excellent, especially at night, and their hearing is phenomenal. They fly silently, hunting by stealth, not speed. There are two families: The dozen or so species of barn owl (p. 49), and the rest.

Strigiformes
owls

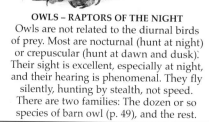

owl

The turkey vulture is the only raptor known to sniff out its food

Cathartidae
New World vultures

condor

Falcons, such as this lanner falcon, have distinctive long, pointed wings

American kestrels (right) and other kestrels are very good at hovering

Large falcons, such as this peregrine, are the fastest birds on earth when they dive down on prey

Caracaras are the only falconids to build nests and to hunt on the ground

Foot of Verreaux's eagle from Africa

Large accipitrids have massively powerful feet

The African harrier hawk is halfway between a harrier and a hawk

Eagles, such as this bald eagle, can see at least twice as far as humans

Egyptian vulture shows the broad, muscular accipitrid tongue

Hooked tip of beak rips into flesh; sides of the beak cut it off

Bald eagles' broad wings enable them to soar effortlessly

ACCIPITRIDS
These are the largest group of raptors: There are 237 species. Hawks, eagles, buzzards, kites, Old World vultures, and harriers are all accipitrids. Their kinship shows in their similar eggs, tongues, and molting patterns. They all build nests. They kill with their feet (falconids often use their beaks as well as their feet). They squirt out their droppings, and falconids let them fall. Most accipitrids have a protective ridge of bone above the eye.

THE FALCONID FAMILY
There are three main groups of falcons: the true falcons (which include kestrels), the little-known forest falcons, and the pygmy falcons, or falconets, smallest of the raptors. The caracaras of the Americas are also related to them, and form part of the Falconidae family, which contains about 60 different species, found all around the world.

Falconidae
falcons and caracaras

kestrel

Accipitridae
hawks, kites, buzzards, eagles, harriers, Old World vultures

goshawk   *kite*   *buzzard*   *golden eagle*

11

Eggs, nests, and hatching

AT THE START of the breeding season, male birds try to show females that they will be good mates. Males perform display flights and bring the females food to prove that they will be able to feed a family. Pair bonds are formed, and the new pairs build nests. Each pair often defends a territory around its own nest to protect its food supply. A few species, however, including several of the kites and vultures, breed in colonies. The smallest birds of prey brood (sit on) their eggs for 28 days before the chicks hatch, the largest for 54 days. Usually, the females brood the eggs. The males bring the females food until the new chicks are big enough to be safely left alone.

Bald eagle egg

Ural owl egg

Peregrine falcon egg

African pygmy falcon egg

ALL SORTS AND SIZES
The above eggs (shown actual size) illustrate the variety of raptor eggs. Owl eggs are much rounder than those of day-flying raptors. Condors and large vultures lay only one egg at each breeding attempt, most eagles two or three, small birds such as kestrels about six, and a few species such as snowy owls lay up to 14.

STARTING A FAMILY
Usually, males and females build their nests together. Male goshawks, however, build three or four nests, by themselves, for females to choose from. Nests are often built in trees or on cliff ledges – in any safe place. Only a few raptors, such as harriers and caracaras, normally build nests on the ground.

Buzzard eggs in nest

ONLY THE STRONG SURVIVE
Some eagles have two chicks, but only one usually survives. If food runs short, the older chick kills the younger. In a few eagles, the older always kills the younger. The chicks of smaller raptors do not usually attack each other, although they do compete for food. If food is scarce, the weakest will die.

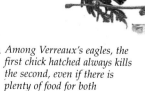

Among Verreaux's eagles, the first chick hatched always kills the second, even if there is plenty of food for both

Larger branches are lodged in tree trunk first, then twigs, then leaves

12

BIGGEST BUILDER
Bald eagles (right) return to the same nests year after year, adding to them each time. They become huge. One, in Florida, was 9.5 ft (2.9 m) wide, 20 ft (6 m) deep, and weighed 2 tons!

WHO'D BE A PARENT?
For ospreys (left), the breeding cycle lasts about nine months from courting displays until the young are independent. This is about average. Most raptors breed every year, if they can. A few very large birds have to look after their chicks for more than a year, so can only breed every other year.

FRAGILE LIFE
Embryos develop inside a protective membrane within the egg. As they do so, an air sac appears at the top, or blunt, end of the egg (right). Where chemicals such as the pesticide DDT get into the food chain, eggs may become infertile or eggshells so thin they crack and the embryos die.

Air sac

Eggs of accipitrids (p. 11), such as this goshawk egg, are blue-green inside

1 *First crack or "pip" in egg*

2 *Baby pecks all around shell, then makes one huge push*

3 *Newly hatched babies rest for several hours before feeding*

BABY BARN OWL BREAKS OUT
When an egg is ready to hatch, the chick taps away for a day or so with a pointed lump called an egg tooth on top of its beak, and "cheeps," perhaps alerting its mother. Finally it makes a crack or hole in the shell. After about another day of tapping, it breaks out. The process can take up to three days.

SECOND-HAND NEST
These kestrel chicks are in a buzzard nest. Owls, falcons, and New World vultures do not build their own nests. Sometimes they take over old nests. More often, they dig a scrape in the surface in some sheltered place. It may be in a cave, on a cliff ledge, in an old barn, or even on the ledge of a skyscraper. Owls may nest in the hollow of a tree.

Growth of the young raptor

Young birds of prey grow very fast, racing through the most vulnerable stage of life. For their first few weeks they just eat, sleep, and grow. Young sparrowhawks are fledged (full-grown and flying) after 26 days and can hunt well enough to feed themselves four weeks later. Larger birds develop more slowly, but even a golden eagle is fledged at two and a half months and independent of its parents three months later. In temperate climates, raptors need to be full-grown and ready to hunt before winter arrives and food becomes scarce. Only a few very large birds in hot countries, such as martial eagles and Andean condors, grow more slowly.

Two-day-old black vulture chick

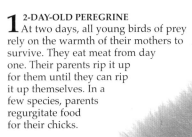

4 2 WEEKS
At two weeks old this barn owl chick is eight times heavier than it was at hatching. Then it weighed about 0.5 oz (14 g) (see p. 13). At two weeks it weighs over 3.5 oz (100 g).

5 3 WEEKS
The chick is nearly ready to stand up. It spent its first weeks sitting on its ankles. It is covered in thicker down, called secondary down, and can keep warm without its mother.

6 6 WEEKS
Feathers are pushing through the skin, and the facial disk is beginning to appear.

7 8 WEEKS
Close to being fully feathered, it practices jumping and wing flapping in the nest to strengthen its muscles. It will be able to fly in about a week.

8 10 WEEKS
It is now fully grown and learning to hunt. It will still rely on its parent for a few weeks more as it learns to hunt well enough to feed itself.

Unlike many birds, raptor chicks (except for owls) have some vision at birth and can take meat from their mother's beak

1 2-DAY-OLD PEREGRINE
At two days, all young birds of prey rely on the warmth of their mothers to survive. They eat meat from day one. Their parents rip it up for them until they can rip it up themselves. In a few species, parents regurgitate food for their chicks.

"Egg tooth" (p.13)

Chicks beg for food, cheeping and raising opened mouths to their parents

2 12-DAY-OLD PEREGRINE
At 12 days peregrines start to get a thick white down. They can now "thermoregulate" – they can keep themselves warm without the heat from their mother. Now she can hunt, with the male, to feed the chicks rapidly-growing appetites. They can eat half their own body weight and more in a day.

Down inadequate to keep chick warm

Juveniles stay near the nest while their parents still feed them, then disperse

Juvenile coloration often has a buff edging

SEVEN-WEEK-OLD PEREGRINE
This seven-week-old peregrine is nearly full grown. Once it has fledged it will be called a juvenile (until it gets its adult plumage). It must then quickly learn to hunt well, or starve. Perhaps 50 per cent of young raptors die in their first year – this varies with food availability from year to year. In temperate climates, many die in their first winter.

4 JUVENILE PEREGRINE
Most young birds of prey are a different color from their parents. This allows them to hunt in the territory of adult breeding pairs, who would drive out other adults. Juveniles are left alone because they are no threat until they are fully adult and ready to breed.

Beak will become strong enough to tear meat after a few weeks

Adults lose the buff edging to the body feathers and become all grey on the shoulders

Young peregrines (this one is one year old) usually have vertical bars or stripes

Horizontal bars and stripes replace the vertical ones of youth

5 ADULT PEREGRINE
Some birds, like kestrels, breed before they are a year old if nest sites and mates are available. Others, like peregrines, start at three or four. Very large birds may not breed until they are six or seven years old. Birds that are over a year old but still in juvenile plumage are called subadults.

Characteristic owl ear hole: a long, thin slit

WHAT AN EARFUL
Owls have bigger ears than other raptors (p. 51), visible in this two-day-old owl chick. Like most raptors, adults rip up food for chicks. A few birds of prey, such as vultures and snake eagles, regurgitate it – snake eaglets pull still-writhing snakes from their parents' mouths.

Feet are soft and weak at this stage; chicks spend their first few weeks sitting on their ankles

How raptors fly

AIRPLANES NEED an engine to push them forward; only their wings will keep them up in the air. Raptors' wings provide both the power to go forward and the "lift" to stay up. As birds flap their wings, the inner part of the wing provides most of the lift, the outer part most of the power. The flight feathers (p. 21) are specially shaped to improve the airflow over the wings and thus the birds' flying ability. The tail is used for steering and for braking: It moves continuously as the bird steers through different air currents. The feathers fan out for a fast turn and open out completely as the bird slows to a stop. The various wing shapes of different raptors enable the birds of each species to fly in a way that suits the terrain in which they live and to hunt effectively.

The rounder wing of the true hawks, or accipiters

FOREST FLYING
Birds of the accipiter family (pp. 40–41) have a longer tail for their body size than most raptors. It enables them to turn fast and stop quickly. Their short, rounded wings give them a fast takeoff speed. This is vital because they must seize their prey before it reaches cover in the woods.

Sparrowhawk

The primary feathers raised in takeoff position

The tail is raised to help the bird become airborne

Legs take awhile to be drawn up out the way

Tail closed when bird is flying in a straight line, opened and tilted when turning

KING OF THE FALCONS
The Arctic gyrfalcon is the largest and possibly the fastest of all the falcons (pp. 58–59). The falcons have long, pointed wings that are not particularly good for soaring or gliding, although they can and do soar, but are perfect for fast flying. The narrowness of the wing reduces drag in the air but also makes it harder to maneuver in wooded areas. Falcon wings are suited to hunting in wide open country.

Powerful legs give added power for thrusting the bird forward and upward

Wing power comes from the breast muscles

The pointe[d] wings of th[e] falcon famil[y]

JUST HANGING AROUND

Eagles, such as this black eagle, are designed for soaring. They are not able to keep up flapping flight for long, and they switch to warm air currents to lift them up, sometimes thousands of feet high, as they watch for prey. It is the raptor version of going up in an elevator. Most big eagles and vultures live either in the mountains and along coastlines, where there are lots of updrafts to soar on, or in hot countries with plenty of thermals (p.18).

Tail fans out to increase lift when bird is soaring

Outer primaries have to be very flexible

Inner primaries bearing the load

The covert feathers protect the wing bone, which is very near the surface

The alula fits in here when not in use

Alula is raised when bird is slowing to a stop

TAWNY EAGLE TAKEOFF

During takeoff, the wings are raised first, then the legs push the bird off in a jump. As the bird jumps, the wings move forward and downward, giving the bird lift and forward motion. This first downbeat is called the power stroke. The primary feathers along the outer part of the wing (pp. 20–21) do most of the work on each downstroke, continuing to give lift and forward direction. On the upstroke, the primary feathers open to move upward more easily, and the secondary feathers on the inner wing maintain the lift.

LAZY FLYER

Condor wings are huge, both long and wide. Condors can soar for hours on rising air currents, looking for dead animals. But they cannot take off easily if full of food or on flat land. On the ground, they have to do a running takeoff to gain speed before trying to become airborne. In their mountain homes, however, they simply open their wings as they take off from the ledges on which they live, and the updrafts do the rest.

Large wing area enables condor to glide on air currents rather than use the more tiring flapping flight

Large birds use legs and feet as air brakes in flight

BRAKING ALULA

This red-tailed hawk is in the landing position: Its body is almost vertical to the ground, rather than horizontal as it is when flying. The wing and tail feathers fan out to slow the bird down. At the top of the wings you can see two "thumbs" standing up; these are the alulas, or "false wings." All birds have them. They smooth out the airflow above the wings at low speeds and prevent the birds from stalling. The flaps, or slats, on airplane wings do the same thing, but not so well.

Styles of flight

All raptors have one of three basic wing shapes. Falcons have slim, pointed wings suited to sustained high-speed flight. Hawks, forest eagles, and other forest birds have short, rounded wings that enable the birds to take off quickly and accelerate rapidly but make fast sustained flight too tiring. Vultures and other large raptors have long, rounded wings suited for soaring. But such wings cannot be flapped as quickly as the shorter wings of hawks and falcons, so the large raptors are not as fast or as agile.

Diving down to link toes

Once the feet are grasped, the birds tumble toward the earth

Bald eagle will turn upside down to meet the other bird's feet

GRAB YOUR PARTNER BY THE CLAW
Some birds have spectacular mating flights. Bald eagles fly really high and then grab the feet of the new mate-to-be, spiral downward together, then release one another. Some observers suggest that this flight also to drive off unwanted eagles from the new pair territory, so that they are not around to compete for food when the pair are feeding their chick

VERTICAL TAKEOFF
Caracaras are related to the falcons but don't have their fast flight. They are, however, much more agile in the air and on the ground. They can even take off and fly vertically for several feet. This may be done to catch insects they disturb while scratching through rotten wood. They spend much of their time on the ground scavenging.

Wings stretched back, moving the bird directly upward

After pushing the caracara upward, the legs dangle

Birds often circle ridges, hoping to pick up a thermal

Bird reaching top of thermal; thermals only last up to a certain height

Raptors often glide from thermal to thermal, traveling without tiring

Migratory raptors ten to avoid large areas of water because the thermals they rely on do not form over water

UPWARDLY MOBILE BIRD OF PREY
The most important aids for soaring birds are thermals. A thermal is a column of warm, rising air. Thermals form as the ground heats up during the course of the day. They form readily over land, but not over water. Raptors can rise effortlessly in thermals, which are vital for migration (pp. 56–57), as well as soaring because they save the birds so much energy. Apart from thermals, raptors' other main sources of rising air currents are coastlines and mountain ridges.

Wings beating fast, tail
starting to fan out as
the bird starts to hover

Kestrels have special, very
flexible necks that keep
their heads still while their
bodies move slightly

The primaries
take the strain

*ing out in the
*pward climb

HELICOPTER BIRD
Kestrels specialize in
hovering as they hunt.
They use the wind to assist
them, flying slowly into the
wind so that their speed and the
wind's speed cancel each other out.
Hovering enables them to stay still and look
for prey over open country, where there are no
perches on which to sit. A few other raptors, such
as buzzards and snowy owls, also hover occasionally.

Machine sketched by Leonardo da
Vinci, one of the earliest attempts
to invent a flying machine

ROLLERCOASTER LIFE
Raptors looking for a mate often do a beautiful
undulating flight to impress prospective
partners. They fly high, fold their wings and
drop like a stone, open the wings, and pull out
of the dive, climb, then close them again in
another dive. The display can also tell other
birds that the displaying bird has claimed the
territory over which it flies and will guard it.

IMPOSSIBLE DREAM
People have always longed to fly like
birds, but even if we could make birdlike
wings for ourselves, human muscles are
far too weak, unlike the muscles of birds
(pp. 22–23). By one estimate, we would
have to have chest muscles 6.5 ft (2 m)
thick to support our weight.

Some kestrels, such as
this European kestrel,
have longer tails for their
size than other falcons do

Head thrust forward
in landing position

Primaries splayed out
and tilted for landing

Wider secondaries
still providing enough
lift to stay airborne

Landing gear
ready for approach

TAWNY LANDING
Often when a bird is
landing it will drop below
the intended perch and glide up
to it. When landing from above the
perch, birds have to put on all the brakes:
The tail fans wide open, the legs are thrown forward,
and the feet are raised. The wings are fanned out as brakes
and the head drops to see where the bird is landing.

The center two tail
feathers, called
"deck" feathers

Wings and feathers

Birds are the only animals with feathers. Feathers serve two purposes. They allow the bird to fly and they keep it warm. They are made of keratin, the same fibrous protein as the scales on reptiles and the hair and nails on mammals. A bird has a variety of different feathers. Most of the visible feathers are contour feathers. The larger ones are flight feathers, found in the wings and tail. Underneath are the soft down feathers, which keep the bird warm. Other feathers have unusual, specialized functions: filoplumes act like eyelashes, semiplumes like a cat's whiskers, and bristles like brushes for preening (grooming the other feathers).

Buzzard (rear view)

Primary feathers

Primary wing covers

Growing wing feathers (left) and tail feathers (right) of young Gabar goshawk

Growing feathers full of blood; when fully grown, feathers are dead, like human hair

ZIP UP YOUR FEATHERS
Feathers have a central shaft with a vane on each side. The vanes are made up of hundreds of tiny barbs (branches) that hook onto each other to create the feather surface. When birds preen themselves, they use their beaks to zip loose hooks back together and to re-waterproof their feathers with oil from an oil gland at the base of their backs.

Vane, made of tiny barbs

Central shaft is called the quill

HOW FEATHERS GROW
Feathers grow from underneath the skin, in lines along the bird's body. While they are growing they are alive and full of blood. The feather is protected at this stage by a sheath. The sheath splits as the feather comes out of the skin. The feather unfurls and the bird preens it into place.

Feather muscle

Bump on skin as feather develops

Emerging feather

Protective feather sheath

Central shaft of growing feather

If part of the feather under skin damaged as it grows, it may remain damaged for bird's life

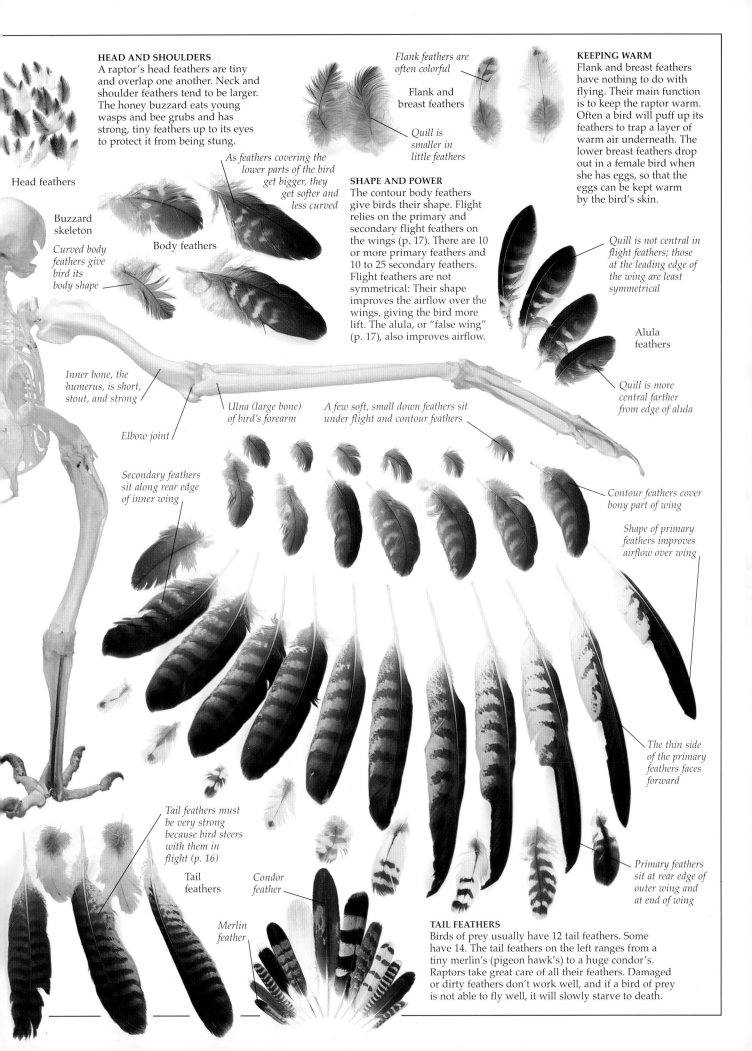

HEAD AND SHOULDERS
A raptor's head feathers are tiny and overlap one another. Neck and shoulder feathers tend to be larger. The honey buzzard eats young wasps and bee grubs and has strong, tiny feathers up to its eyes to protect it from being stung.

Head feathers

Buzzard skeleton

Curved body feathers give bird its body shape

Body feathers

As feathers covering the lower parts of the bird get bigger, they get softer and less curved

Flank feathers are often colorful

Flank and breast feathers

Quill is smaller in little feathers

KEEPING WARM
Flank and breast feathers have nothing to do with flying. Their main function is to keep the raptor warm. Often a bird will puff up its feathers to trap a layer of warm air underneath. The lower breast feathers drop out in a female bird when she has eggs, so that the eggs can be kept warm by the bird's skin.

SHAPE AND POWER
The contour body feathers give birds their shape. Flight relies on the primary and secondary flight feathers on the wings (p. 17). There are 10 or more primary feathers and 10 to 25 secondary feathers. Flight feathers are not symmetrical: Their shape improves the airflow over the wings, giving the bird more lift. The alula, or "false wing" (p. 17), also improves airflow.

Quill is not central in flight feathers; those at the leading edge of the wing are least symmetrical

Alula feathers

Quill is more central farther from edge of alula

Inner bone, the humerus, is short, stout, and strong

Ulna (large bone) of bird's forearm

Elbow joint

A few soft, small down feathers sit under flight and contour feathers

Contour feathers cover bony part of wing

Secondary feathers sit along rear edge of inner wing

Shape of primary feathers improves airflow over wing

The thin side of the primary feathers faces forward

Tail feathers must be very strong because bird steers with them in flight (p. 16)

Tail feathers

Condor feather

Merlin feather

Primary feathers sit at rear edge of outer wing and at end of wing

TAIL FEATHERS
Birds of prey usually have 12 tail feathers. Some have 14. The tail feathers on the left ranges from a tiny merlin's (pigeon hawk's) to a huge condor's. Raptors take great care of all their feathers. Damaged or dirty feathers don't work well, and if a bird of prey is not able to fly well, it will slowly starve to death.

Inside a bird of prey

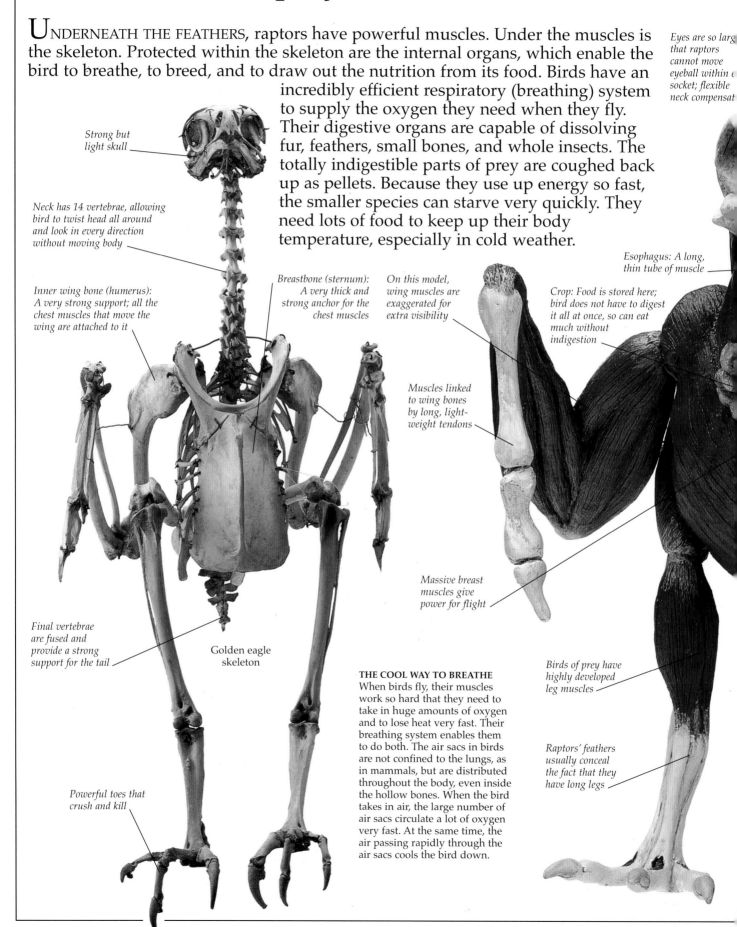

UNDERNEATH THE FEATHERS, raptors have powerful muscles. Under the muscles is the skeleton. Protected within the skeleton are the internal organs, which enable the bird to breathe, to breed, and to draw out the nutrition from its food. Birds have an incredibly efficient respiratory (breathing) system to supply the oxygen they need when they fly. Their digestive organs are capable of dissolving fur, feathers, small bones, and whole insects. The totally indigestible parts of prey are coughed back up as pellets. Because they use up energy so fast, the smaller species can starve very quickly. They need lots of food to keep up their body temperature, especially in cold weather.

Strong but light skull

Neck has 14 vertebrae, allowing bird to twist head all around and look in every direction without moving body

Inner wing bone (humerus): A very strong support; all the chest muscles that move the wing are attached to it

Breastbone (sternum): A very thick and strong anchor for the chest muscles

On this model, wing muscles are exaggerated for extra visibility

Final vertebrae are fused and provide a strong support for the tail

Golden eagle skeleton

Powerful toes that crush and kill

Eyes are so larg that raptors cannot move eyeball within e socket; flexible neck compensat

Esophagus: A long, thin tube of muscle

Crop: Food is stored here; bird does not have to digest it all at once, so can eat much without indigestion

Muscles linked to wing bones by long, light-weight tendons

Massive breast muscles give power for flight

Birds of prey have highly developed leg muscles

Raptors' feathers usually conceal the fact that they have long legs

THE COOL WAY TO BREATHE
When birds fly, their muscles work so hard that they need to take in huge amounts of oxygen and to lose heat very fast. Their breathing system enables them to do both. The air sacs in birds are not confined to the lungs, as in mammals, but are distributed throughout the body, even inside the hollow bones. When the bird takes in air, the large number of air sacs circulate a lot of oxygen very fast. At the same time, the air passing rapidly through the air sacs cools the bird down.

ones of spine are largely fused, so
tle muscle is needed along back

eight is concentrated
ound center of gravity

*Posture of model is
slightly unnatural*

Side view of
golden eagle's
muscles

A PELLET A DAY

All birds of prey produce pellets of
undigested material, such as this,
every day or so. Scientists use these
pellets to find out what birds have
been eating. Owl pellets are the most
revealing because their stomachs are
not as good at digesting small bones
as are the stomachs of diurnal
(day-flying) raptors.

Falcon pellet

*Falcons and other
day-flying raptors
digest most of the
small bones of their prey*

DIGESTION TIME

When birds of prey eat, the meat goes into the crop
first, except in owls, which do not have a crop.
Then it goes into the stomach. There the
unwanted parts, such as feathers, are
packed into a ball to be regurgitated
the next day, and the rest is digested.

Golden eagle model
showing muscles (left)

Golden eagle (right)

POWER LIFTER

Nearly half the weight of a bird
of prey is taken up by its muscles.
The breast, or pectoral, muscles are
the largest. They do the work of
making the bird fly. Because the
big flight muscles are all in the
chest, the wings are kept light
and the weight of the bird is
kept central, making it more
stable in the air. The leg
muscles are also very
powerful, to grip and
crush quarry.

Feet and talons

A RAPTOR'S MOST IMPORTANT TOOLS ARE ITS FEET. Their size, shape, and strength show what it is capable of catching. For example, kites can be large birds – red kites are about the size of a small eagle – but their tiny feet only allow them to catch frogs, beetles, mice, and young rabbits. The peregrine, on the other hand, is smaller than the kite but has enormous feet, enabling it to catch birds almost its own size. Vultures have weak feet, because dead animals don't struggle very much, whereas the martial eagle of Africa can catch and kill young ostriches and small antelopes! If you want to know what a bird of prey eats, look at its feet.

TALONS AND TOES
Talons, which would be toenails on our feet, can be huge on large eagles. In some female eagles, the inner and back talons can be as long as your thumb.

Feathers fanned out for landing

This bone is the foot bone, although it appears to be part of the leg

These bones are the toes, and the talons are the toenails

GOLDEN EAGLE FOOT
Birds, like dogs, walk on their toes. The bird "foot" has become an extension of the leg. It helps to absorb the shock of landing and to push up when taking off. The ankle is halfway up the leg. The knee is hidden under the feathers at the top of the leg.

Falcons' feet are large but not particularly strong

SAKER FALCON FOOT
Falcons often strike their prey at high speed. They even occasionally close the foot into a fist and punch the quarry. They don't usually kill prey with the sheer crushing power of their feet, but may finish the kill with their beaks.

Very large back talon

BLACK EAGLE
With its enormous feet, the African black eagle, or Verreaux's eagle, catches the nearest living relative of the elephant! It is a much smaller relative. In fact, the rock hyrax looks like a giant guinea pig. The eagle's big, powerful feet are ideal for grabbing these very stout, rounded animals.

BLACK VULTURE FOOT
The New World vultures have feet more like a big chicken's than a bird of prey's. These feet have very little grip or power, but they are great for standing on all day. The feet of Old World vultures are more powerful although still relatively weak for raptors of their size.

Soft feathering on owls' feet and legs helps to keep them warm and silent

Vultures' talons do not need to be curved because they are used for walking, not for killing prey

OWL FOOT
Most owls except the fishing owls have feathered toes for silent flying and landing. Owls, and ospreys, have reversible outer toes that can be pointed backward as well as forward. They perch, and grasp things, with two toes forward and two back. The rest of the birds of prey perch and grasp with three toes forward and one back.

When owls' feet are relaxed, they have three talons forward, one back

AFRICAN FISH EAGLE FOOT
The osprey and all the fish eagles have very scaly feet, and when they grasp a slippery fish it cannot wriggle away. The bottoms of their legs are bare, not feathered, so they don't have to fly around with wet feet.

SPARROWHAWK LEG
Sparrowhawks tend to catch small birds, such as sparrows, hence their name. They often snatch birds from the air. They have long, thin legs and thin toes, with needle-like talons, perfect for grasping their small, elusive prey. Raptors that catch more powerful prey, such as rabbits and other sizeable mammals, have relatively shorter, stronger leg bones.

The knee joint

The ankle joint

Talons more curved than other eagles'

Long, thin bones give extra reach

Birds perch and walk on their toes, not their feet

This foot is larger than a human hand

25

Hunting techniques

Eagle eating
a snake

SOME RAPTORS THAT LIVE in open country fly high, survey a wide area, then swoop fast. Eagles glide down quickly to take prey on the ground, and falcons dive even faster to catch birds in midair. Harriers hunt differently: They fly low and slow, looking and listening for quarry in the undergrowth. Owls tend to do this too. Many raptors, especially those that live in wooded areas or towns will often "still-hunt," that is, hunt from perches, sprinting out from cover when prey comes around the corner. Some – goshawks, for example – fly close to the ground, using hedges and trees as cover, to surprise prey. A few birds of prey, such as secretary birds and caracaras, hunt on the ground. As they walk along, they flush out prey.

STILL HUNTING
Buzzards, such as this red-tailed hawk, are very good at still hunting. A buzzard will sit and watch and wait as a rabbit wanders, until that rabbit strays just too far from its hole, which is its last mistake. Birds such as kestrels that normally hunt in flight may still-hunt when they have no chicks to feed, or are tired, because still hunting uses less energy.

Nictitating membrane (p. 30) often sweeps across to protect eye as bird attacks

The perch must be inconspicuous; many raptors have a favorite perch that they use frequently

Some raptors flit from perch to perch as they hunt (p. 40)

Feet can lock onto prey so powerfully that sometimes raptors find it hard to release prey

DROPPING IN FOR A BITE
Some birds of prey, like this red-tailed hawk, will catch anything they come across. The red-tailed hawk, or red-tailed buzzard as it is called in Europe, will hunt for small prey like this chipmunk but can also manage a fully grown rabbit that weighs as much as the buzzard does. Other raptors, such as the snail kite (p. 8), eat one particular prey. Individual birds may develop their own specialties: Some peregrine falcons wait on cliff ledges to ambush birds flying past.

Tail is spread out to act as a brake

FISHING EAGLES

Fish eagles, like this white-bellied sea eagle, and ospreys, fishing buzzards, and fishing owls live near seas, lakes, and rivers and catch fish. Except for ospreys, whose hunting technique is all their own (p. 36), these birds usually sit on a high perch watching the water for fishes feeding on the surface. A low-angle dive allows them to plunge their feet into the water and snatch a fish.

Primary feathers fan out to keep bird from stalling as it brakes rapidly

Hawks spot potential prey

Eagle surveys wide areas as it spirals high on thermals (p. 18)

VIEW TO A KILL

Large eagles (except forest eagles, p. 42) need wide, open spaces to fly and maneuver in as they hunt. They often soar, looking for tiny movements, such as a rabbit flicking an ear or a hare scratching its side, and then stoop with deadly intent. At other times they may still-hunt.

One hawk swoops down to flush the prey out of cover

Other hawks move into position to ambush prey

STOOP TO CONQUER

All large falcons inhabit open country. There is no cover, so their prey can see them far away, and they may face a long chase to catch it. To help them get extra speed, they climb high and stoop (dive) on their quarry when it is far from cover. If they miss, they climb and stoop again.

Eagle drops down on its quarry

Quarry driven into open

ALL IN THE FAMILY

Most raptors are solitary hunters. Sometimes breeding pairs hunt together. A few species work in teams. Harris's hawks hunt in family groups of up to six. Several birds may tackle the prey at once. If the prey is in cover, one or more birds may try to flush (frighten) it into the open. Occasionally the birds take turns harassing a likely prey, until it is confused, exhausted, and helpless. Together the group can tackle larger prey than one bird could on its own, such as jackrabbits twice as heavy as the largest Harris's hawk.

The kill

Prey and feeding

SOME RAPTORS WILL EAT ANYTHING; others are specialist feeders. The snail kite (p. 8) only eats snails, and the bearded vulture (left) eats mostly bones and marrow (the nutritious substance inside bones). Insects are very important to many birds of prey: 12 species eat only insects, 44 species eat mostly insects, and another 100 species occasionally eat insects. A few birds of prey even eat fruit as well as meat; one is the palm-nut vulture, which is named after its favorite food. The small insect-eating birds must eat their tiny prey frequently, but many of the larger birds survive on one or two kills a day and can spend the rest of their time sitting and digesting. Vultures may have to look for a long time for food, so they gorge themselves when they can: an 11-lb (5-kg) griffon vulture can eat nearly 4.5 lb (2 kg) in one meal. Most birds of prey feed alone or with their families, but vultures and kites will gather in large groups at a sizable food source, such as a dead buffalo or a town dump.

SOME RAPTORS WILL EAT ANYTHING; others are specialist feeders. The snail kite (p. 8) only eats snails, and the bearded vulture (left) eats mostly bones and marrow (the nutritious substance inside bones). Insects are very important to many birds of prey: 12 species eat only insects, 44 species eat mostly insects, and another 100 species occasionally eat insects. A few birds of prey even eat fruit as well as meat; one is the palm-nut vulture, which is named after its favorite food. The small insect-eating birds must eat their tiny prey frequently, but many of the larger birds survive on one or two kills a day and can spend the rest of their time sitting and digesting. Vultures may have to look for a long time for food, so they gorge themselves when they can: an 11-lb (5-kg) griffon vulture can eat nearly 4.5 lb (2 kg) in one meal. Most birds of prey feed alone or with their families, but vultures and kites will gather in large groups at a sizable food source, such as a dead buffalo or a town dump.

When a caracara is upset or excited, blood rushes to skin above beak, which turns red

Empty crop

PICK OF THE CROP
All the day-flying birds of prey have crops (p. 22). Their food goes into the crop when they eat and is digested later. As they eat, the crop gradually bulges out. In most raptors the crop is hidden by feathers, but in caracaras it is bare and looks very odd when full.

BEARDED WONDER
Bearded vultures are named for the beard like feather tufts on their faces. They eat bones. Small bones they swallow whole, large bones they drop onto rocks from about 200 ft (60 m), sometimes more than 20 times, until they break.

Primary feathers are black, rest of bird is white

Black vultures can fold the feathers up on their bare necks when they are cold, or down when they are feeding so that blood doesn't get all over them

Vultures brace themselves on their strong legs to rip off tougher pieces to eat

BRING A FRIEND
It is thought that if black vultures such as these find a carcass whose skin is too tough for them to tear open, they will go and find a larger king vulture and lead it to the carcass. The king vulture rips it open and feeds, and the black vultures can eat too.

Skin above beak is usually yellow

Full crop; contrast empty crop of caracara on left

Caracaras scavenge dead rabbits and most other dead creatures

NOT WELCOME AT THE FEAST

Some raptors, such as this Cooper's hawk, "mantle" their food. That is, they spread their wings out above it as they eat, hiding it because many creatures, including other raptors, might try to steal it. Raptors usually carry prey away to a safe place to eat it if it is small enough to lift.

Wings outspread to hide food look like a cloak or mantle, so the action of spreading them to hide food is called "mantling"

Cooper's hawks eat small mammals and birds, such as this quail

Egg-shaped stones are preferred for throwing at ostrich eggs

SEASONS OF PLENTY

Each year, the bald eagles of North America's Pacific coast have a huge banquet as the salmon come upriver, lay their eggs, and die (p. 37). Other raptors benefit from occasional surges in the numbers of their prey, such as locust and mice plagues. Snowy owls and rough-legged hawks lay significantly more eggs when their main prey, lemmings, have a population explosion. The letter-winged kite of arid inland Australia does not breed until the rains are good and its main prey, the long-haired rat, is abundant; then it raises several broods one after the other.

Nostrils, or nares, are not see-through in Egyptian and other Old World vultures, unlike New World vultures (p. 31)

Pacific salmon die after they have spawned (laid their eggs), so the bald eagles just have to drag their bodies out of the river

BIRD-BRAIN EXTRAORDINAIRE

Various raptors will eat eggs if they find them, but Egyptian vultures are the only ones that use a tool to do so, and are among the few known tool-using birds. To break into an ostrich egg, they pick up small rocks and throw them at the egg until it breaks open. Smaller eggs are picked up and thrown at the ground. In South Africa, where ostriches are farmed commercially, ostrich farmers shot and poisoned Egyptian vultures; none breed there anymore. Other ingenious raptors include bearded vultures. As well as dropping bones from a height, they also drop tortoises to break open their shells.

Ostrich eggs are the largest eggs in the world

Heads and senses

HUNTING OTHER ANIMALS is the hardest way to find your food. One aid for birds of prey is their excellent eyesight – at least two or three times as good as ours. In one test, a buzzard saw small grasshoppers 330 ft (100 m) away; a human could only see them 100 ft (30 m) away. Some species may see even better – up to eight times as well as people. Raptors also hear very well, especially owls (p. 51) and some harriers. The only bird of prey that uses its nose to find food is the turkey vulture. It's hard to sniff out supper while flying at high speed.

EYE STORY
The eyes of a eurasian buzzard (skull above) can be as big as an adult human's eyes, although the human weighs 50 times as much!

Nictitating membrane protects and cleans the eye

PROTECTIVE EYEBROW
Birds such as the ferruginous hawk have a very obvious eyebrow called the supra-orbital ridge (p. 11). The ridge may shade the eyes from the sun when hunting or protect the eye from injuries when hitting prey or crashing through trees in a chase.

EARS AND SPEED
The ear hole is small but important. Sound is used for calling, recognizing mates, and locating prey. Falcons, such as the peregrine (skull at left), rely less on hearing than do owls and some harriers, which fly slow and low, listening for prey.

Rather small brain tilts to fit into back of skull

Hole for the ear, normally covered in feathers

THE BEAUTIFUL BITE
Falcons, such as this saker falcon, have large heads for their size. All falcons have an extra serration on each side of the beak. Called the toral tooth, it is used, with the feet, for killing quarry. Other birds of prey do all their killing with their feet, saving their beaks for eating.

"Toral tooth" to kill prey

Eyes and beak take up a lot of room; brain is not so big

EYE WIPER
The eye of this Verreaux's eagle looks clouded over, but there is nothing wrong. The cloudy surface is in fact a third eyelid called the nictitating membrane. This membrane is a tough, clear skin that can flick across the eye and keep it clean without stopping the bird from being able to see. It is often closed on impact with prey to protect the eye.

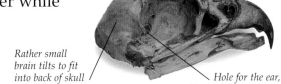

The eagle can see at least twice as far as a human, probably farther

THE USES OF THE TONGUE
Raptors, like dogs, pant to lose heat – as this golden eagle is doing. They breathe through a hole halfway along their tongues. And they use their tongues to hook food back from the tips of their beaks so that they can swallow it.

Little is known about raptors' sense of taste; some captive birds show definite likes and dislikes

Brain area of the bird of prey

GREAT EYES, NO BRAINS
It is hard to know exactly how far an eagle can see. There is no doubt, however, that a golden eagle can see a rabbit at least 1 mile (1.6 km) away, and probably much more. Its brain is not so impressive. The cleverest birds of prey are the vultures.

Brown snake eagle skull

HEAD TURNER
Birds of prey have such enormous eyes that they cannot move them in the sockets. Instead, they can see all around by turning their heads with their long, flexible necks. They like to look at the world from many angles and will even turn their heads to look at life upside down.

Young African fish eagles have brown and white heads; adults' heads are pure white

This subadult bird's head is gradually turning white

Small brain

Eyes face forward, so that their fields of vision overlap (this is called binocular vision), which enables the bird to judge distance

HUNTERS' EYES FACE FORWARD
Raptors, such as this black kite, have forward-facing eyes, like other hunting animals (including humans). This gives them the ability to judge depth and distance, which is vital for successful hunting (pp. 50–51).

VOICE OF AFRICA
African fish eagles are very noisy and use their loud calls to welcome their mates. Raptors use their voices in many ways, from chicks begging their parents for food, to the excited calls made during aggressive encounters, to the softer noises of courtship.

White-backed vultures are not really bald; the head and neck are covered in a fine down

Piercing eye of vulture scans wide areas for carcasses, from high above

Supra-orbital ridge

Crest is only half-extended

NO NEED FOR KNIFE AND FORK
Vultures, such as this white-backed vulture, have very strong necks and beaks to help them tear through the tough skin of large animals. Big vultures, such as the lappet-faced vulture in Africa and the Andean condor, can break through the skin of dead buffaloes and whales! If smaller vultures find such big animals first, they have to wait for the larger birds to start the feast before they can join in. The smaller birds' beaks are not strong enough to cut through such tough skin.

Turkey vultures are probably the only raptors to smell out their food

Nares (nostrils) are completely see-through

SENDING SIGNALS
Many birds of prey have a crest. No one really knows why some birds have crests, but it may be so that they can signal their moods to other birds of the same kind. A raised crest probably means the bird is angry. Crests vary in length. Changeable hawk eagles, such as this one, have short crests.

A NOSE FOR FOOD
The only bird of prey known to have a good sense of smell is the turkey vulture. In American forests, it flies very slowly over the tree canopy trying to locate dead animals by smell. Other species of vulture wait for the turkey vulture to find food and then follow it down to eat.

Thin but powerful beak

People need aids such as binoculars; human sight is far weaker than that of an eagle

Skeletons

White-tailed sea eagle

IN SOME BIRDS OF PREY, the skeleton weighs less than the feathers. For example, the skeleton of a male European sparrowhawk is only about 11 percent of its total body-weight. This lightness is necessary if the birds are to fly – the heaviest flying bird in the world weighs only 35 lb (16 kg), and fast-flying, agile birds weigh a fraction of that. Many of the larger bones are hollow and filled with air to make them light. At the same time, the skeleton has to be strong enough to anchor and support the powerful flying muscles and protect the internal organs. It needs to be rigid enough to hold the muscles in place yet flexible enough to withstand heavy stresses.

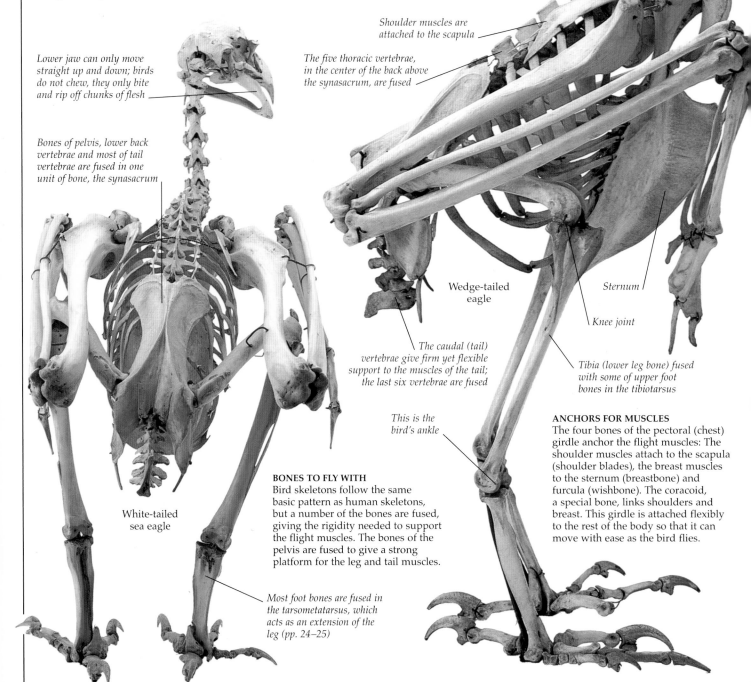

Wedge-tailed eagles have 14 cervical (neck) vertebrae

The coracoid links the sternum and the shoulder area

Shoulder muscles are attached to the scapula

Lower jaw can only move straight up and down; birds do not chew, they only bite and rip off chunks of flesh

The five thoracic vertebrae, in the center of the back above the synasacrum, are fused

Bones of pelvis, lower back vertebrae and most of tail vertebrae are fused in one unit of bone, the synasacrum

Wedge-tailed eagle

Sternum

Knee joint

The caudal (tail) vertebrae give firm yet flexible support to the muscles of the tail; the last six vertebrae are fused

Tibia (lower leg bone) fused with some of upper foot bones in the tibiotarsus

This is the bird's ankle

White-tailed sea eagle

BONES TO FLY WITH
Bird skeletons follow the same basic pattern as human skeletons, but a number of the bones are fused, giving the rigidity needed to support the flight muscles. The bones of the pelvis are fused to give a strong platform for the leg and tail muscles.

ANCHORS FOR MUSCLES
The four bones of the pectoral (chest) girdle anchor the flight muscles: The shoulder muscles attach to the scapula (shoulder blades), the breast muscles to the sternum (breastbone) and furcula (wishbone). The coracoid, a special bone, links shoulders and breast. This girdle is attached flexibly to the rest of the body so that it can move with ease as the bird flies.

Most foot bones are fused in the tarsometatarsus, which acts as an extension of the leg (pp. 24–25)

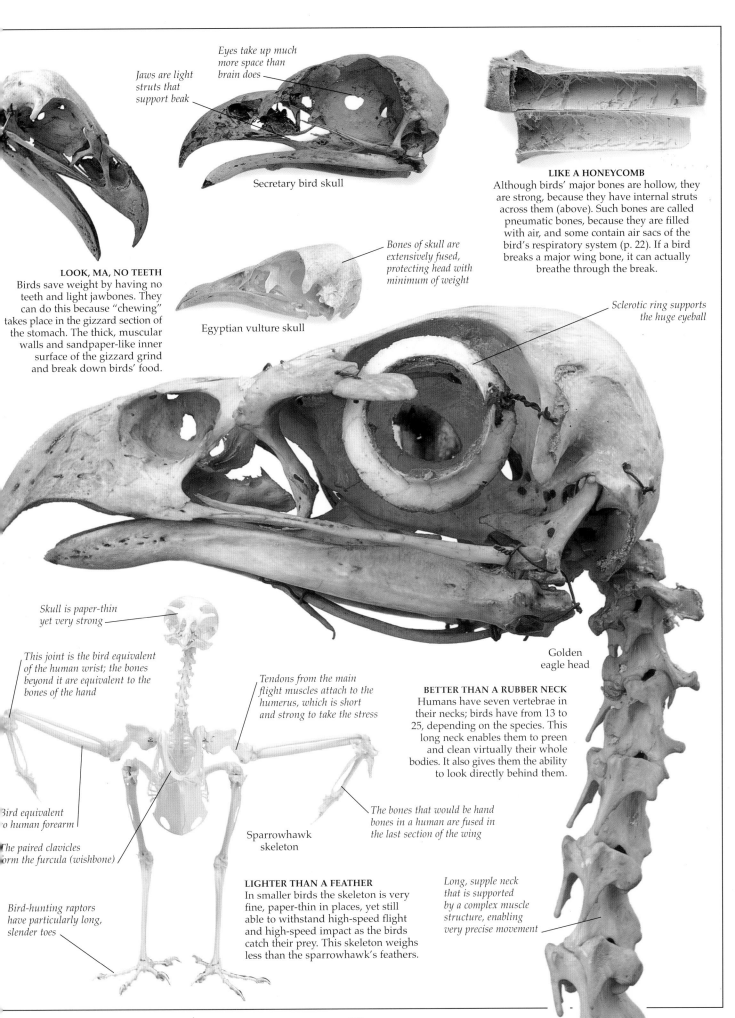

Jaws are light struts that support beak

Eyes take up much more space than brain does

Secretary bird skull

LIKE A HONEYCOMB
Although birds' major bones are hollow, they are strong, because they have internal struts across them (above). Such bones are called pneumatic bones, because they are filled with air, and some contain air sacs of the bird's respiratory system (p. 22). If a bird breaks a major wing bone, it can actually breathe through the break.

Bones of skull are extensively fused, protecting head with minimum of weight

LOOK, MA, NO TEETH
Birds save weight by having no teeth and light jawbones. They can do this because "chewing" takes place in the gizzard section of the stomach. The thick, muscular walls and sandpaper-like inner surface of the gizzard grind and break down birds' food.

Egyptian vulture skull

Sclerotic ring supports the huge eyeball

Golden eagle head

Skull is paper-thin yet very strong

This joint is the bird equivalent of the human wrist; the bones beyond it are equivalent to the bones of the hand

Tendons from the main flight muscles attach to the humerus, which is short and strong to take the stress

BETTER THAN A RUBBER NECK
Humans have seven vertebrae in their necks; birds have from 13 to 25, depending on the species. This long neck enables them to preen and clean virtually their whole bodies. It also gives them the ability to look directly behind them.

Bird equivalent to human forearm

The paired clavicles form the furcula (wishbone)

Sparrowhawk skeleton

The bones that would be hand bones in a human are fused in the last section of the wing

Bird-hunting raptors have particularly long, slender toes

LIGHTER THAN A FEATHER
In smaller birds the skeleton is very fine, paper-thin in places, yet still able to withstand high-speed flight and high-speed impact as the birds catch their prey. This skeleton weighs less than the sparrowhawk's feathers.

Long, supple neck that is supported by a complex muscle structure, enabling very precise movement

Neck tucked into ruff of feathers to keep warm

Vultures

Vultures are the garbage collectors, or scavengers, of the raptor world. They prevent disease by eating dead animals before they decay. In Africa, they eat far more meat than all other predators put together – an estimated 27,500 tons (25 million kg) each year on the Serengeti plains alone. Vultures, especially big vultures, are good at soaring but bad at flapping flight (pp. 16–19), so most live in hot places or in mountainous areas. There are two separate groups: New World vultures in the Americas and Old World vultures elsewhere. Both groups range from huge birds of 22 lb (10 kg) or more to small species of only 4–7 lb (2–3 kg). The largest, condors, have 10-ft (3-m) wings.

10-ft (3-m) wingspan

CONDORS
The Andean condor (above) soars above the Andes mountains of South America. Some glide right across to the Pacific coast and scavenge dead whales. The California condor (p. 59) recently became extinct in the wild, but birds bred in captivity are now being released to re-establish the species.

New World vultures urinate over their legs and feet, perhaps to cool themselves

HOME WITH A VIEW
Many vultures breed in the mountains where predators cannot reach them, as at Vulture Rock in Spain (above). Some species nest alone in caves, others in large groups called colonies.

Juveniles have dark brown plumage, adults have white

Bright yellow face; neck not bare, unlike most vultures

OLD WORLD
Old World vultures are related to kites and eagles, whereas New World vultures are related to storks, and only distantly to the other birds of prey. The smallest of the Old World vultures are Egyptian vultures (above). There are two kinds: The Indian race has yellow beaks and the European and African races have black beaks.

Wings outstretched to keep its balance

NEW WORLD
The turkey vulture is the smallest of the New World vultures and has the largest range (lives over the widest area). It is found from southern Canada to Argentina. It has a better sense of smell than other birds of prey (pp. 30–31), which it uses to sniff out dead animals in the forests and woodlands.

Turkey vulture gets its name from its red face

Neck feathers can be pulled down like a ruff when the bird is hot or feeding, and pulled up when it is cold

New World vultures have chicken-like feet

The tail sticks up when it is doing its bouncing walk

The dropped head can mean different things, including aggression

DINNER PARTY: NO JACKET REQUIRED
Vultures gather in dozens to eat large carcasses.
In Africa up to six different species may gather
at once, plus rival scavengers such as marabou
storks. Some vultures appear to be there for
social reasons and don't actually eat. A large
group of vultures can strip an antelope carcass
bare in 30 minutes, and a cow in three hours.

Eurasian
griffon skull

*Marabou storks
eat dead meat*

*Upper mandible
fixed to the skull*

WATCHER IN THE SKY
Vultures have excellent (daylight) eyesight.
As they soar, they watch for signs of death,
and watch one another. If one bird starts to
drop, its neighbors will follow, then their
neighbors, and so vultures can come in
from nearly 200 miles (300 km) away to
a carcass. Eurasian griffons such as this
belong to the family of Old World vultures
called griffon vultures, or just griffons.

*Lower mandible moves,
much like our jaw*

COMMON BUT CLEAN
White-backed vultures are the most
common in Africa. They have bare
heads and necks, like most vultures,
because they put their heads inside
carcasses. Feathered heads would
get very dirty. All vultures love to
bathe and, after they have fed,
will fly long distances to wash.

*Huge wings give vultures
their soaring ability*

*A white-backed vulture
can eat 2.2 lb (1 kg) of
meat in two minutes*

THESE FEET WERE MADE FOR WALKING
Some vultures like to walk. In fact, the
American black vulture (below) literally
bounces along on strong legs. When
hunting for small dead animals, like
crabs or baby turtles, it spends much of
its time on the ground. Black vultures'
legs and feet have evolved to make
them more sure-footed
than other vultures.

*Black vultures can
run or bounce along
at quite a fast rate*

Ospreys and fish eagles

OSPREYS ARE UNIQUE. Found in most parts of the world, they are perfectly adapted for catching fish, and eat almost nothing else. To help them grip their slippery food, their talons are extra-curved, and they have scales on the soles of their feet and specially adapted toes (p. 24). They soar high above the water to spot their prey, then dive steeply down to seize it, and they are the only raptors that will go completely underwater to catch a fish. The eight species of fish eagle are not so specialized. They do catch fish, and, like ospreys, have extra-curved talons and scaly soles to their feet. But they also scavenge a lot, and will eat just about anything they can find or catch. Unlike ospreys, fish eagles usually catch fish by "still-hunting" – quietly sitting and waiting for fish to swim by, then diving (at a shallower angle than ospreys) and dipping their feet into the water to scoop up a surface-swimming fish. Fish eagle species include the bald eagle and the huge Steller's sea eagle.

BORN TO FISH
Ospreys have long legs for catching fish under the water and their outer toes can be swung backwards to hang on to slippery prey better (p. 25). Their plumage tends to be more waterproof than other raptors'. They can even close up their noses to keep water from rushing in.

Osprey's wings sweep back in the final dive into the water

ARC OF A DIVER
Ospreys usually take fish close to the water surface. They can plunge into the water, however, leaving only the tips of their wings showing. They soar, circle, and even hover over water as they look for quarry, then dive in, throwing their feet forward to snatch the fish. After resting a few moments on the water, they pull out with strong, horizontal wing beats.

Fish is held with its nose facing the front to reduce drag

SYMBOL OF AMERICA
The bald eagle was chosen as the national emblem of the United States in 1782. Benjamin Franklin, statesman and scientist, disapproved of the choice because bald eagles steal food from others. He believed the turkey should become the emblem. The eagle won the day. In recent decades it became endangered as a result of persecution and pollution. Great efforts were made to save the symbol of the nation, and the species is now much recovered.

Eagle holds olive branch to symbolize peace

Other foot holds arrows to symbolize war

Ospreys have narrow heads, with no bony ridges above their eyes

Sturdy nests withstand storms on exposed coasts

FAMILY HOME
Ospreys use the same nest year after year, and even generation after generation. It can become very big as it is added to each year. All sorts of materials are added to it, even bones, old rope, cardboard, and plastic bags, although these can entangle and kill the growing young. Some ospreys nest in reed beds, or on the ground on treeless islands.

These eagles have loud and raucous voices

VARIED DIET
The white-bellied sea eagle lives along the coasts of India, southeast Asia, and Australia. As well as fish, it hunts rabbits, fruit bats, gulls, water birds, even poisonous sea snakes. In some places it now suffers from the effects of the lethal pesticide DDT (p. 13).

WAITING FOR THE FEAST

Every year, Pacific salmon swim upriver, lay their eggs, and die, and bald eagles gather to feed (p. 29) on them. It is possible to see 2,000 of them on one river in Alaska in this season. Fish eagles' broad wings enable them to fly carrying prey heavier than they are. Bald eagles can carry 7 lb (3 kg) salmon, and one even flew away with a 15 lb (7 kg) deer. Steller's sea eagles can probably carry even heavier loads.

The eagles just sit and wait for the salmon to die

Steller's sea eagle is instantly recognizable by its enormous beak

THE EAGLE HAS LANDED, AGAIN

The white-tailed sea eagle is one of the largest species of eagle. It has been hunted and persecuted by humans for centuries. The last white-tailed sea eagle in Great Britain was shot in 1916 and the species became extinct there. Gradually, people have become more aware of their responsibilities to the environment, and in the 1960s white-tailed sea eagles were released into the wild on a remote Scottish island. The bird is still rare in Britain, but its numbers are growing.

THE BIG-BEAKED BIG BROTHER

Steller's sea eagles are the largest of all the fish-eating birds of prey. They live on the coast of Russia and China and feed mainly on Pacific salmon. They will also catch large birds, such as geese, mammals such as hares, and even young seals. Like all fish eagles, Steller's sea eagles lay two to three eggs and rear more than one young per clutch (unlike some of the true eagles, p. 12).

Supra-orbital ridge

This juvenile bird does not yet have the full adult plumage

Powerful beak can tear through tough fish skin with ease

Sea eagle swallows bones with the flesh

Strong feet with rough scales hold the slippery catch

Tail slowly turns white as eagle reaches adult breeding age

Salmon is the favorite food of many northern eagles

Kites and harriers

KITES ARE VERY GRACEFUL fliers, easily recognized in flight by their forked tails. There are 33 species. The largest, the European red kite, weighs 12 times as much as the smallest, the South American pearl kite, which weighs about 3.5 oz (100 g). Many of the smaller species eat insects, others hunt for larger quarry, some are scavengers, and some even fish. The 13 species of harriers, and three related species, all have huge wingspans and light bodies, which allow them to fly very slowly while looking and listening for potential prey. All tend to live in open areas: marsh, grasslands, or farmed land.

Swallow-tailed kite in flight

Male drops food to female

AEROBATIC LUNCH
The male harrier does not usually bring food to the nest. Instead, he calls to the female, who flies to meet him. He flies over her and drops food, which she catches with her feet and brings back to the nest while he hunts again.

African harrier hawk has a large crest and bare face

Color of back feathers is different for juveniles and adults

Harriers often nest in reeds, tussocky grass, or even standing crops

NO HIGH-RISE HERE
Most harriers build nests on the ground, like the marsh hawk above. The females make the nest with sticks, dry reeds, and grass. Harriers usually lay three to four eggs but can have up to ten when food is plentiful. Kites usually build messy nests in trees.

ADAPTABLE BIRD
Black kites are found in many areas of the world (p. 58). They have a varied diet, including mice, rats, fish, frogs, insects, small birds, and carrion. Like many kites, they fly in large flocks where food is abundant, but nest alone. Like all kites, they often catch food in midair, eating it from their feet as they fly.

Long thin legs and toes are ideal for pushing into cracks and holes to find food

RAPTOR RESEMBLANCES
The African harrier hawk and its faraway relative, the crane hawk of South America, are medium-sized raptors that resemble the harriers. They, too, have huge wings and low body weight. They fly very slowly through woodlands, looking for tree holes or rock crevices to raid. The harrier hawk group has double-jointed legs. The ankle can bend either way as the hawk gets its talons into a hole to snatch a baby bird out of its nest or some other creature out of its hiding place.

CLOSE RELATIONS
Yellow-billed kites are the African subspecies of the black kite. They are a slightly different color and have a yellow bill (beak).

Kites can twist and turn in an amazing fashion

Most kites have a forked tail; in some species, much more forked than this

Red kite has a pale iris

Harriers sometimes fly at a height of less than 3 ft (1 m) as they hunt

SLOWLY DOES IT
Harriers hunt by flying low and slow over marsh, moor, and grasslands, methodically zigzagging to cover all the ground over which they are hunting. They listen for sounds in the grass – some even have a facial disk to sharpen their sight and hearing, like owls. They eat prey up to the size of a small rabbit.

SUCCESS STORY
In developed countries, a number of raptors suffered huge declines in recent decades due largely to pesticides and other features of modern farming. A number of these species have recovered greatly. The red kite was once the most common kite in Britain, then was reduced to a small, declining population in Wales. It has now been reintroduced into England and Scotland, and is thriving.

Large flocks of kites will scavenge for food in town dumps

NOT FUSSY, OR FEARFUL
Kites are not afraid of humans – in Africa, some have learned to snatch sandwiches from people's hands. Kites will go into town dumps and garbage heaps to find scraps to eat. However, they run the risk of picking up poisonous food, or getting bits of plastic or string caught around them.

Reddish color of feathers gives this species its name

Long tail aids slow flying

Kites are easy to identify in flight by their forked tails

Hawks and buzzards

North American Swainson's hawks, like other hawks, often hunt from man-made perches such as telephone poles

TRUE HAWKS (GENUS *ACCIPITER*) are fast-flying and very agile, with short, rounded wings that help them twist and turn through trees as they chase after quarry. They also have long tails that help in steering and act as brakes, enabling them to stop quickly. Buzzard hawks (genus *Buteo*) are very adaptable birds. They live and hunt in a wide range of environments, especially part-wooded and cultivated land. They are less agile than accipiters, with longer, broader wings and shorter tails. They scavenge where they can and take a variety of prey. Like all buzzards, they soar a lot, watching out for food from high in the sky.

LOOK AT THOSE LEGS

There are about 20 speci of buzzards, or buteos, around the world, including the long-legge buzzard (left). All buzza are stocky, with thick leg and powerful feet, becau they mainly catch mammals (p. 25). For mo buzzards, rabbits and rodents are the main pre

BEST OF HUNTERS

In medieval Europe, the goshawk, a true hawk, was known as the "cook's bird," not because it was flown by cooks but because it caught so much food for the larder. Sparrowhawks were less popular because they catch smaller prey, but were still flown. Buzzards were probably used to train apprentice falconers, as buzzards are slower than hawks, and easier to train.

Sparrowhawk plucks feathers from blackbird before eating it

Hawklike wings and tail give great agility, but Harris' hawks tend to fly more slowly (and use their brains more) than true hawks

DON'T EAT THE FEATHERS

Like many other raptors, hawks pluck the feathers from their prey before eating. They often have "plucking posts" near their nests, where they take their kill. True hawks are divided into the (larger) goshawks and the (smaller) sparrowhawks. There are about 20 species of goshawk, and about 25 species of sparrowhawk. Goshawks hunt both "fur and feather" – both mammals and birds; sparrowhawks usually catch small birds. Hawks often hunt by flitting from perch to perch, skimming the ground between trees so that prey will not spot them.

Harris's hawks have relatively short primary feathers

Hawks can take relatively big prey: female sparrowhawks catch wood pigeons, which are heavier than they are, as well as blackbirds such as this

Hawks often use hedges and trees as cover as they fly toward prey, only "breaking cover" and showing themselves at the last moment

FEEDING THE KIDS
Numbers of Eurasian buzzard (above) rise and fall with prey populations. In Britain, the number of breeding buzzards fell dramatically when the disease myxomatosis killed off most rabbits, then rose tenfold in 12 years as rabbit numbers recovered.

HAWK OR BUZZARD?
The Harris's hawk is an unusual bird because it falls between the hawk and buzzard families. Its scientific name is parabuteo, which means "like a buzzard." It has the characteristic hawk shape, with long tail and short, rounded wings. It resembles buzzards in its relaxed temperament (hawks tend to be high-strung). It is unusually sociable. It hunts in groups (p. 27) and breeds cooperatively: Parents are helped in rearing chicks by other Harrises in the group.

False wing helps with stopping and low-speed flight (p. 17)

Harris's hawks are also called bay-winged hawks because of the brown color on the top of their wings

The mammal-hunting hawks have strong legs; the smaller sparrowhawks, which prey on birds, have thinner, less strong legs with very long toes

Eagles

AROUND THE WORLD the eagle is seen as the king of the birds. Many kings, nations, armies, and empires have taken eagles as their symbols. There are over 40 species of eagle, and several distinct groups. The forest eagles include the crowned eagles of Africa, Philippine eagles (p. 56), and South American harpy eagles (p. 59), which are probably the most powerful of all raptors. The true eagles live in open country. Some, such as golden eagles, wedge-tailed eagles, and martial eagles, can have wingspans of over 8 ft (2.5 m). Forest eagles have shorter, more rounded wings and longer tails than true eagles. Snake eagles have thick scales on their legs and feet, that protect them from snakebite, and short, strong toes that enable them to grasp the snakes.

CHILD SNATCHER?
Many eagles eat carrion. Some have been seen feeding on prey much bigger than anything they could kill. This is why myths developed about eagles carrying off calves, sheep, and even human babies. For all the stories of eagles carrying off children, there is no verified record of any eagle killing a child.

JUNGLE EAGLE
Most forest eagles belong to the subfamily of hawk eagles. The African hawk eagle (right) is one. Hawk eagles are so called because their shape is similar to that of hawks. Like hawks, they can turn very fast and so can hunt amid thick trees. Sadly, a number of hawk eagles are becoming rare as the forests that they live in are steadily cut down.

Striped breast feathers act as camouflage when eagle sits in trees

COMMON PIRATE
Tawny eagles are among the most numerous of eagles. Like many other eagles, they mainly scavenge, eating from carcasses and even human garbage. They often act as "pirates," chasing other raptors that have just caught prey and stealing it.

All true eagles have feathers down to their toes, as do some forest eagles

Eagles that have feathers down to their toes are sometimes called "booted eagles"

IMPERIAL SYMBOL
Eagles have been the symbols of many great empires, including ancient Rome, the Russia of the Czars, and the Austrian Hapsburg empire. Roman legions used to carry eagle standards as their symbols and rallying points (above). To lose the legion's eagle was the worst of all possible disasters.

Birds often pick a dead branch high up as a lookout point

Eagle spreads wings to make itself look larger and more threatening

Warthog is defending its baby from the eagle

BABY WARTHOG SNATCHER
The giant martial eagle (above), the biggest in Africa, is powerful enough to kill jackals and small antelopes, let alone baby warthogs. Martial eagles, which live on the plains of Africa, are among the largest of all eagles. Some have wingspans of over 8 ft (2.5 m). Forest eagles never have as big wings as the biggest of the true eagles. They have to maneuver through jungles or forests at high speed as they hunt, so have shorter wings and longer tails.

Nictitating membrane protects and cleans eye

FAMILY HOME
Golden eagle pairs return to the same nest sites year after year to raise their young (right). Only bald eagles build larger nests (p. 13). Good nesting sites stay in use: When one pair stops breeding, another uses the nest. Golden eagles reach maturity at five, coming into adult plumage, ready to breed.

Chicks cheep to stimulate their mother to feed them

Brown plumage of young bateleur changes gradually into adult plumage

Golden eagle gets its name from the (relatively) gold-colored feathers on the back of its head and neck

ACROBAT OF THE AIR
A dull brown juvenile bateleur eagle (above) grows into a brightly colored adult (left), reaching maturity at seven. Bateleurs are closely related to the snake eagle family but eat mainly carrion. They were given the name bateleur, which in French means balancer or tightrope walker, because they are so acrobatic in the air.

Fork halfway along tongue helps bird to pull food back into its throat

Some golden eagles have wingspans of more than 2.5 m (8 ft)

RELIGIOUS RAPTOR
The eagle is a religious symbol in many cultures, including the North American Indian. In some religions an eagle represents the sun or a god – often a sky god. In Christianity the eagle came to be a symbol of John the Evangelist (above), one of the first disciples of Jesus Christ.

Contour feathers (p. 21) give shape to wing

Golden eagles help farmers by killing rabbits and other animals that damage crops

Stocky build is characteristic of golden eagles

This 4.5 lb (2 kg) rabbit will last the 9 lb (4 kg) eagle for two days

MODERATE EATER
Golden eagles live in the tundra areas of the northern hemisphere. Like most eagles, they kill prey much smaller than they are, although they may feed off large dead animals. The biggest exception is Africa's crowned eagle. Crowned eagles have been known to kill antelopes weighing up to 45 lb (20 kg).

The secretary bird

SECRETARY BIRDS have been described as long-legged marching eagles. Their long legs make them look almost like storks, but they have the hooked raptor beak and, like all birds of prey, they kill with their feet. They live in Africa south of the Sahara, in almost every region that can offer them grasslands, desert edges, or farmed land in which to live. They also need a flat-topped tree to nest in. About 4 ft (1.2 m) high, they weigh 4.5–9 lb (2–4 kg), and have a wingspan of 6.5 ft (2 m) or more. They cannot live in forests because it is too tricky for them to take off and fly amid the trees, and they avoid very thick, tall grass. They flush prey out by walking, not flying, through the long African grass, and then they kill it by stamping on it, with great force and accuracy. Famous for killing snakes, they also eat a wide variety of insects, small animals, and birds.

THE REASON FOR THE NAME
One story is that the long feathers on secretary birds' heads were reminiscent of European secretaries with quill pens behind their ears (above). Or the name may come from the Arabic *saqr-tair* – "hunter bird."

Two-week-old secretary bird

The same bird at six weeks old

THE YOUNG SECRETARY BIRD
When first hatched, young secretary birds have huge heads. Their legs grow so fast that the scales can't keep up, and in the first few days the old scales split off and new scales grow again and again. They cannot stand up until almost full-grown, which means that they cannot fall out of the nest until ready to fly, or at least glide. Secretary birds are valuable to farmers because they kill rodents and poisonous snakes. Most African nations have laws to protect them, but some people hunt them illegally.

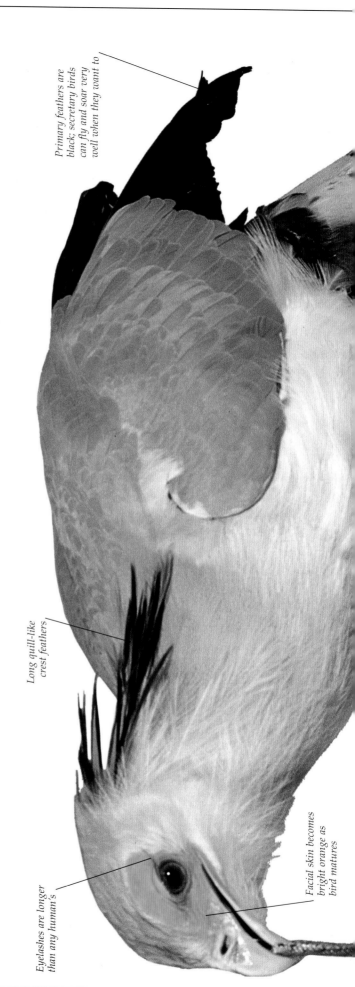

Primary feathers are black; secretary birds can fly and soar very well when they want to

Long quill-like crest feathers

Eyelashes are longer than any human's

Facial skin becomes bright orange as bird matures

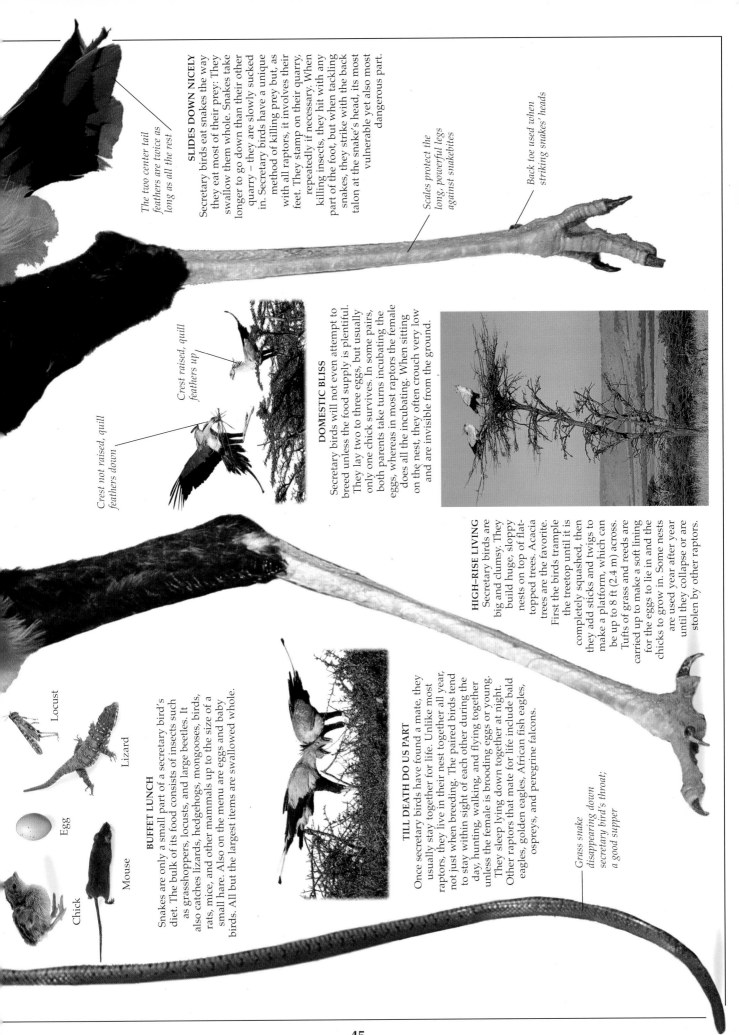

SLIDES DOWN NICELY

Secretary birds eat snakes the way they eat most of their prey: They swallow them whole. Snakes take longer to go down than their other quarry – they are slowly sucked in. Secretary birds have a unique method of killing prey but, as with all raptors, it involves their feet. They stamp on their quarry, repeatedly if necessary. When killing insects, they hit with any part of the foot, but when tackling snakes, they strike with the back talon at the snake's head, its most vulnerable yet also most dangerous part.

The two center tail feathers are twice as long as all the rest

Scales protect the long, powerful legs against snakebites

Back toe used when striking snakes' heads

Crest not raised, quill feathers down

Crest raised, quill feathers up

DOMESTIC BLISS

Secretary birds will not even attempt to breed unless the food supply is plentiful. They lay two to three eggs, but usually only one chick survives. In some pairs, both parents take turns incubating the eggs, whereas in most raptors the female does all the incubating. When sitting on the nest, they often crouch very low and are invisible from the ground.

HIGH-RISE LIVING

Secretary birds are big and clumsy. They build huge, sloppy nests on top of flat-topped trees. Acacia trees are the favorite. First the birds trample the treetop until it is completely squashed, then they add sticks and twigs to make a platform, which can be up to 8 ft (2.4 m) across. Tufts of grass and reeds are carried up to make a soft lining for the eggs to lie in and the chicks to grow in. Some nests are used year after year until they collapse or are stolen by other raptors.

BUFFET LUNCH

Snakes are only a small part of a secretary bird's diet. The bulk of its food consists of insects such as grasshoppers, locusts, and large beetles. It also catches lizards, hedgehogs, mongooses, birds, rats, mice, and other mammals up to the size of a small hare. Also on the menu are eggs and baby birds. All but the largest items are swallowed whole.

Locust

Lizard

Egg

Mouse

Chick

TILL DEATH DO US PART

Once secretary birds have found a mate, they usually stay together for life. Unlike most raptors, they live in their nest together all year, not just when breeding. The paired birds tend to stay within sight of each other during the day, hunting, walking, and flying together unless the female is brooding eggs or young. They sleep lying down together at night. Other raptors that mate for life include bald eagles, golden eagles, African fish eagles, ospreys, and peregrine falcons.

Grass snake disappearing down secretary bird's throat; a good supper

The falcon family

THE BIG FALCONS – sakers, lanners, peregrines, and gyrfalcons – are probably the fastest-flying of all the birds of prey, and when they stoop (dive), the fastest birds in the world (p. 58). They live in open country, such as desert edges, tundra, moor, and grasslands. There are also various smaller true falcons, including kestrels. Forest falcons are small, little-known birds that live in tropical rainforests. The smallest members of the falcon family, and the smallest raptors of all (p. 58), are pygmy falcons. Caracaras don't look or behave much like falcons, but they belong to the same family (p. 11). They come from Latin America and spend much of their time on the ground, scratching under logs and stones searching for food.

Game bird being struck in midair

Falcon stoops after strike but turn to grab the p

CATCHING PREY
Many falcons catch their prey by flying high above it, stooping dow at high speed behind it, and then striking it in midair. Sometimes a falcon will grasp the prey in the air This is called "binding to it." Often the falcon will hit the prey as it dive past, then either pick up the dead bird on the ground or catch it in midair before it hits the ground.

The hobby is a small falcon, so agile it can catch swifts in midair

Caracaras have a different wing shape from that of falcons

THE ODD RELATIVES
Caracaras may not behave much like falcons, but scientists tell us that they are closely related. Rather than hunting in the air, they scavenge like vultures. They are clever birds and will often annoy campers in the Andes by stealing food from their camps.

STRIPES OF YOUTH
A falcon's juvenile plumage has downward vertical stripes on the chest, and the shoulders and back feathers have buff edging. This plumage usually goes in the first molt, but it allows the bird to hunt in adult territory before it grows adult plumage (p. 15). Falcons born in hot countries often look much paler than those hatching in cooler ones because the sun bleaches out the color in the feathers.

Notch, or tooth, on falcon's beak

Heavily striped breast of immature lanner

Juvenile male lanner

FLYING HUNTER
Lanners live in some parts of Europe and the Middle East, and all over Africa except for the rainforest and the Sahara. They catch small birds in the air and also insects, small mammals, and reptiles. They are numerous in Africa but rare in Europe. A program in Israel to breed them and release them into the wild is doing well.

Adul male lanne

Spots of adult plumage

Short tail means falcons can't maneuver as well as hawks

Side view of juvenile to show back feathers

Side view of adult to show back feathers

Peregrine falcon nesting on a cliff ledge

Kestrels are a common sight in many towns

CHOOSING A HOME
Like owls, falcons don't build nests. Smaller falcons and forest falcons use abandoned nests or holes in trees. Larger falcons tend to use ledges on cliffs, rocks, or buildings. They build scrapes in the soil or dirt on the ledge, then lay their eggs.

Young members of the rarest species of falcon in the world, the Mauritius kestrel

TAKING TIME TO LOOK AROUND
The 13 species of kestrel around the world are all able to hover (p. 19), some better than others. This enables them to "perch" in midair, giving them time to spot small animals on the ground. Other falcons are flying swiftly past on their way to catch birds, so the kestrels have less competition for snatching ground prey.

BIRD ABOUT TOWN
Kestrels, and some other falcons, have learned that high-rise buildings are a little like cliffs, with ledges and alcoves that make good nesting places. They have also learned that where humans live, so do many other animals that the falcon can use as a food source. There are problems, though – young birds may get run over before they learn to deal with traffic.

NOWHERE TO FLY TO
Mauritius kestrels almost became extinct recently, mainly because of the destruction of the forests on their home island. A breeding and release program has saved them, for the time being. Small populations of any raptor are always vulnerable, especially if they live on islands (p. 59).

Contour feathers have buff edges in immature plumage

Subadult female lanner

Juvenile stripes are lost in the first molt, after which the bird is subadult (p. 15)

Falcons' toes are even longer than hawks' toes

UNISEX FEATHERS?
In some raptors, males and females have differently colored plumage. Usually the difference doesn't show until the birds have their adult plumage. American kestrels, or sparrow hawks, are one exception: The difference is obvious as soon as they have feathers. This sub-adult female lanner (left) is pretty much the same color as a subadult male. The only real difference is that the female is usually about a third heavier than the male. This is about average for falcons (p. 9).

Adult female lanner

Crop area is often less marked than the lower breast

This dark bar is called the mustachial strip

INDIVIDUAL MARKINGS
You can tell a lot about a bird from its feathers. Within each species, there is a certain amount of variation in plumage. Individuals differ, and in many species so do birds from different regions. Some lanners are more heavily marked than others and some have a redder color to the back of the head. Adult lanners from southern Africa have a pink breast with no markings; northern lanners tend to be very heavily marked.

Tail feathers are used in steering, and as brakes

47

Owls

WHEN THE NIGHT COMES, owls take over from the other raptors. They hunt by stealth, flying slowly, softly, silently to surprise their prey. They rely on their ears more than their eyes to catch their prey. Most, though not all, are night (nocturnal) hunters, or hunt at dawn and dusk. They range in size from the tiny elf owl of the U.S., which weighs only 1.4 oz (40 g), up to the eagle owl of Europe, which is a massive 6.5 lb (3 kg). Most owls rest during the day. Their feathers are in dull colors to camouflage them from possible predators in the day and from possible prey at night. The different groups of owls hunting at night fill all the hunting roles of the diurnal (daytime) birds of prey except for scavenging (carrion is hard to see at night) and the fast flying and diving of the falcons.

Baby owls are soon able to swallow their food, such as this mouse, whole

MIDNIGHT HOWLER
The tawny owl has the most famous of owl calls in Europe – "too-witt-too-woo." It also makes a shrill "kee-wick" noise late at night. Like many other raptors, it likes to catch its prey by still-hunting (pp. 26–27): It sits very still and quiet, listening and looking for movement, then it pounces.

SILENT EAGLE OF THE NIGHT
Owls fly on large, silent wings. Their feathers have a fine down all over, and the leading edges of the outer flight feathers are serrated like a comb. This gives a soft, frayed fringe that deadens the noise of their wingbeats so that prey don't hear them coming. Owls are not particularly fast or agile fliers; they rely on surprise as they float through the night. The largest of all owls are the various Eagle owls.

All feathers are covered in a fine down to aid silent flight

Bengal eagle owl

Breast feathers give warmth in cold weather; their mottled coloring provides camouflage

Eagle owls have feathered toes, which help protect their feet from bites

HOOTING BOOBOOK
The boobook owl gets its name from the hooting noise it makes. Several other kinds of owls are named after the sounds they make. For example, there is a screech owl, and even an owl called a saw-whet owl, which is said to make a noise like a saw being sharpened. Owls call to attract mates or mark out their territory.

Boobook owl's coloring serves as camouflage during the daytime

Baby owls are covered in a fluffy down to keep them warm

Barn owls help farmers by killing mice and rats

BABY OWLS

Baby owls, such as these eagle owls, can often be of very different sizes in the same brood. The mother bird starts sitting on the eggs almost as soon as she has laid the first one, so there can be a large gap between the oldest baby and the youngest. This is called asynchronous hatching. Owls grow a little more slowly than other birds of prey of similar size.

FARMER'S FRIEND

Barn owls are a little different from other owls: They have a more pronounced facial disk (p. 51), enabling them to have even better sight and hearing and making them particularly nocturnal. There are about 12 species, found around the world. They often live on farms because there are lots of mice and rats to hunt. They are known for living in barns, but any place secure, weatherproof, and quiet will do – on top of bales of hay, in hollow trees, even on the ground.

Snowy owl's white feathers camouflage it in snow

DAYTIME OWL

Most owls prefer to hunt at night, or at dawn and dusk, but many also have to hunt in the day when raising chicks. The snowy owl and other owls that live in the Arctic have no choice about daylight flying: In the summer the days are so long there is no night.

Owl's huge eye is vulnerable to damage

Secondary feathers

Primary feathers

ON THE DEFENSIVE

Owls can be very fierce when defending themselves or their nests. To make themselves look fierce, they spread their wings and turn them around so the back faces the front (left). This makes them look much bigger than they really are. The pearl-spotted owlet has two white patches on the feathers at the back of its head. The patches look like eyes and stare out at any potential hunter.

For many owls, a vole such as this is a favorite food

DOWN IN ONE

Owls, more than other raptors, like to swallow their prey whole if it is small enough. Most owls eat rodents, especially rats, mice, and voles. Many owls, especially small ones, live on insects. Fishing owls eat fish; spectacled owls eat crabs; eagle owls catch rabbits, hares, and even day-flying raptors as they rest at night.

The life of owls

Owls do not build their own nests. They use holes in trees or abandoned buildings or barns, even bridges – or they take over abandoned nests. One species, the ferocious great horned owl, sometimes even takes over inhabited hawks' nests, killing the occupants. Owls tend to be fairly secretive birds. They hide during the day because other birds might attack them, knowing that owls may kill them at night as they sleep. Even tiny birds like chickadees harass them and try to drive them away whenever they are seen. Crows and magpies will kill owls if they can.

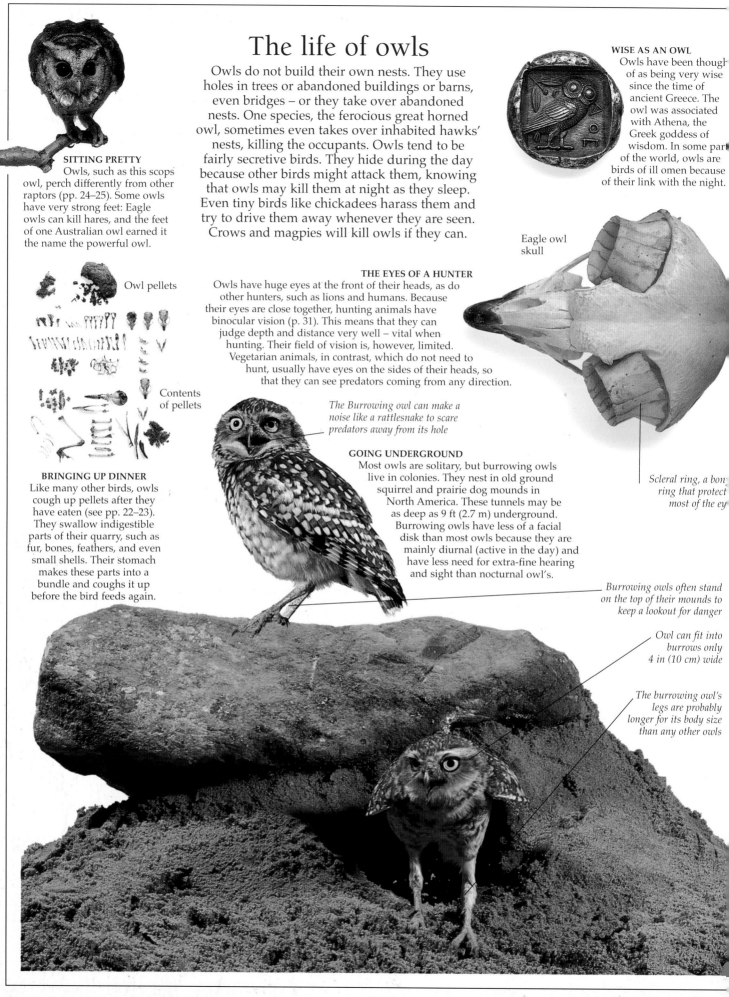

SITTING PRETTY
Owls, such as this scops owl, perch differently from other raptors (pp. 24–25). Some owls have very strong feet: Eagle owls can kill hares, and the feet of one Australian owl earned it the name the powerful owl.

Owl pellets

Contents of pellets

BRINGING UP DINNER
Like many other birds, owls cough up pellets after they have eaten (see pp. 22–23). They swallow indigestible parts of their quarry, such as fur, bones, feathers, and even small shells. Their stomach makes these parts into a bundle and coughs it up before the bird feeds again.

WISE AS AN OWL
Owls have been though of as being very wise since the time of ancient Greece. The owl was associated with Athena, the Greek goddess of wisdom. In some part of the world, owls are birds of ill omen because of their link with the night.

Eagle owl skull

THE EYES OF A HUNTER
Owls have huge eyes at the front of their heads, as do other hunters, such as lions and humans. Because their eyes are close together, hunting animals have binocular vision (p. 31). This means that they can judge depth and distance very well – vital when hunting. Their field of vision is, however, limited. Vegetarian animals, in contrast, which do not need to hunt, usually have eyes on the sides of their heads, so that they can see predators coming from any direction.

The Burrowing owl can make a noise like a rattlesnake to scare predators away from its hole

GOING UNDERGROUND
Most owls are solitary, but burrowing owls live in colonies. They nest in old ground squirrel and prairie dog mounds in North America. These tunnels may be as deep as 9 ft (2.7 m) underground. Burrowing owls have less of a facial disk than most owls because they are mainly diurnal (active in the day) and have less need for extra-fine hearing and sight than nocturnal owl's.

Scleral ring, a bon ring that protect most of the ey

Burrowing owls often stand on the top of their mounds to keep a lookout for danger

Owl can fit into burrows only 4 in (10 cm) wide

The burrowing owl's legs are probably longer for its body size than any other owls

Owls' senses

Owls are famous for their ability to see in the dark. They cannot see in total darkness but need only the tiniest bit of light. Their hearing is even better: In tests, barn owls have caught mice in total darkness by hearing alone. Most birds have small ear openings; owls have long vertical slits that can be almost as long as the head (p. 15). In some owls, one of the ears is much higher on the bird's head than the other. This makes it easier for the owl to work out where a sound is coming from, and so to hunt down the animal that made it.

Another way to look at life

Owls, such as this juvenile barn owl, can turn their heads in every direction

Starting face backward, an owl can turn its head over 360°

If they start face forward, owls can turn their heads 270° each way

Ear tufts have nothing to do with ears; they are probably used to signal moods, such as anger, excitement, and fear

Facial disk channels light and sound into eyes and ears

WHAT A DISH
One of the things that helps owls, such as this Bengal eagle owl, to see and hear so well is the shape of their faces. They have a facial disk or dish, which funnels all available light and sound into their eyes and ears – somewhat like a satellite dish. This facial disk is usually marked by a ring of small bristle-type feathers.

Tawny owl with head turned

Mouth is much larger than size of beak would suggest

Birds of prey in history

BIRDS OF PREY have always seemed magical and fascinating to human beings. They are important symbols in ancient cultures all over the world and in many religions. The eagle, always seen as the king of the birds, represents authority, strength, victory, and pride, and it is linked with the sun, royalty, and gods, especially sky gods. The owl may symbolize wisdom, or, because it is a bird of the night, it may be linked with death and ill fortune, its cry an evil omen. More practically, people have hunted with raptors since ancient times. As far as is known, falconry was first practiced in Central Asia about 4,000 years ago. It has been popular for many centuries in China, India, the Middle East, and Europe.

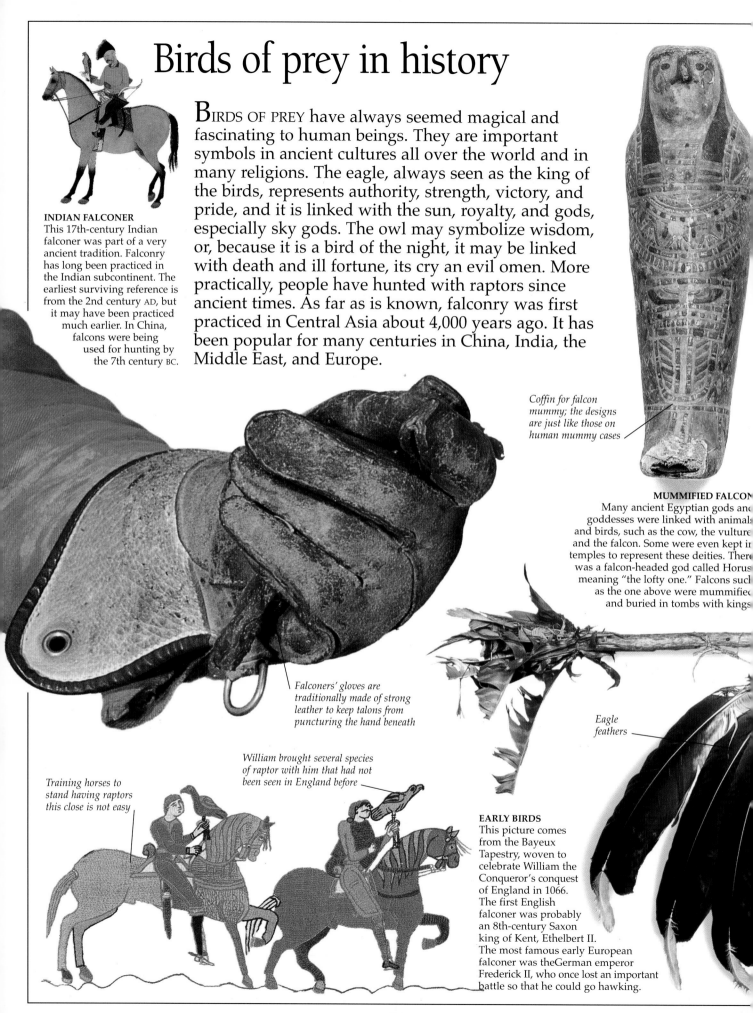

INDIAN FALCONER
This 17th-century Indian falconer was part of a very ancient tradition. Falconry has long been practiced in the Indian subcontinent. The earliest surviving reference is from the 2nd century AD, but it may have been practiced much earlier. In China, falcons were being used for hunting by the 7th century BC.

Coffin for falcon mummy; the designs are just like those on human mummy cases

MUMMIFIED FALCON
Many ancient Egyptian gods and goddesses were linked with animals and birds, such as the cow, the vulture, and the falcon. Some were even kept in temples to represent these deities. There was a falcon-headed god called Horus meaning "the lofty one." Falcons such as the one above were mummified and buried in tombs with kings.

Falconers' gloves are traditionally made of strong leather to keep talons from puncturing the hand beneath

Eagle feathers

Training horses to stand having raptors this close is not easy

William brought several species of raptor with him that had not been seen in England before

EARLY BIRDS
This picture comes from the Bayeux Tapestry, woven to celebrate William the Conqueror's conquest of England in 1066. The first English falconer was probably an 8th-century Saxon king of Kent, Ethelbert II. The most famous early European falconer was the German emperor Frederick II, who once lost an important battle so that he could go hawking.

*Painted plaster mask
for a falcon mummy*

*The Cooper's hawk
is almost vertical as
it comes in to land*

*This was worn on a
lip plug, which was
inserted through a hole
made in the bottom lip*

FACIAL CHARM
Because raptors have always
been seen as special and precious,
jewelry and statues have often
been made in their image. Eagle
heads like this one were made as
lip ornaments by the Mixtecs of
Mexico, who made most of the
gold work for the famous Aztec
empire. Birds of prey have also
often been featured in objects
made for ritual religious use.

*The actual
falcon mummy*

*Hunting straps, a
modern invention*

HAWK MAGIC
To have a wild bird
such as this Cooper's
hawk choose to fly
toward you and land
on your fist is a magical
experience. There is a bond
between falconer and bird that
has given falconry an appeal to
people in many different cultures,
throughout history. Today, although
falconry is no longer needed to provide
food, its appeal is as strong as ever.

*The Cooper's hawk throws
its legs up high to cushion
the impact of landing*

EAGLES AND THE SPIRIT
The bald eagle and golden eagle
have long been objects of worship
to North American Indians.
Eagles are still important in the
ceremonies of many Native
American peoples. Their
feathers have often been
collected and used in many
decorative ways, most
famously on headdresses.
This eagle feather wand
(left) was waved to the
music of drums and
rattles in the eagle dance
of the Cherokee tribe.

DESERT SPORT
Falconry has been
popular in the Arab
world for centuries.
Originally, as elsewhere,
it was a means of
catching food, such as
bustards and desert hares. Now it is a
sport. The falcons are often transported
to the hunting grounds in airplanes, and
the chase is more likely to be followed
in Land-Rovers than on camels.

Training a bird of prey

16th-century English falconer putting a hood on a falcon

Once, birds were trained to catch prey for humans to eat, but today falconry is a popular sport. It is practised in many parts of the world, including the United States, Europe, the Arab world, and Central Asia. Birds that are flown range from great eagles to tiny sparrowhawks. The first step in training a bird is to let it know that the trainer is not an enemy, but a friendly source of food. Next, the bird is asked to jump or hop onto the trainer's gloved fist for food. The distance is then increased until the bird is flying 330 ft (100 m) or so to the trainer's fist. Throughout these exercises, the bird is attached to the falconer by a long, fine string. When the bird responds well to the falconer's calls, it can be flown free, and the falconer and bird can begin to hunt together.

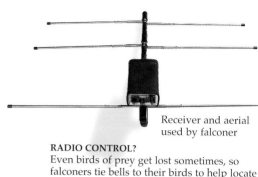

Receiver and aerial used by falconer

RADIO CONTROL?
Even birds of prey get lost sometimes, so falconers tie bells to their birds to help locate them. Nowadays, they can use radio tracking equipment, called telemetry. A very small transmitter (left) is attached to the bird before it starts flying. This transmitter sends out a "bleep" that can be heard by a special receiver (above) to a distance of 15 miles (25 km) in perfect weather conditions, most often about 4 miles (6 km). The signal can sometimes be blocked by hills or woods.

Transmitter and bells are clipped to bird

The hood "hoodwinks," or fools, the bird into thinking that it is night, and so time to be calm and still

Peregrine falcon

Larger part of jesses removable for safe flying

Smaller part of jesses attached to bird's legs

Anglo-Indian hood

Hawk master swivel

Old brass swivel

Hawk and falcon swivel

Sparrowhawk swivel

WEIGHT WATCHERS
Probably the most important piece of falconry equipment is the scales. Falconers know the best "flying weight" of each bird and weigh their birds each day before flying them. If the bird is too heavy, it may not be hungry enough to want to hunt, or it may fly off into a tree to rest rather than come back. If it is too light, it will feel weak and sick. So it must be at the right weight for the falconer to be sure it will come back.

Dutch hood

Weights must be accurate

Blocked hood

FURNITURE FOR BIRDS
The trained bird has to wear various pieces of equipment, known as "furniture," so that its handler can control it. It wears leather straps, called jesses, on its legs so that the falconer can hang on to it – a little like the collar on a dog. The falconer holds long straps attached to the jesses. The straps are threaded through a metal swivel so that they don't become tangled if the bird twists around. If the bird is on an outside perch, it is tethered by a leash threaded through the ring on the swivel.

The falconer's knot has to be tied one-handed, as the other hand is carrying the bird

Arab-style hood

Falconer's bag, with pockets for meat and equipment

Dummy rabbit for hawks or buzzards to chase

Rabbit lure

Plume on hood acts as handle when putting hood on or taking it off

Spare pair of jesses kept on bag

Falconer's glove

Leash should be wrapped neatly, otherwise it might tangle the bird if it jumps or twists around

Old pair of wings with meat attached, used in training falcons

Belt keeps falconry bag in place

PORTRAIT OF A FALCONER

It takes a long time to learn how to be a falconer. A mistake can cause the loss or even the death of a bird. The bird needs to be flown every day while it is being trained except when it is having a rest to molt. An experienced falconer can have a falcon or buzzard flying free in two or three weeks and an eagle in six weeks, although the bird will still have much more to learn.

Creanse (training line)

Rabbit leg

Larger bits of meat are used to get the birds' attention, smaller bits are given as rewards

Knife

Clippers

Bits of beef

Lure

Right-handers hold birds on left hand, left-handers the other way round

Items falconers carry in their bags

Around the world

MANY OF THE RAPTORS which breed in the northern hemisphere fly south for the winter (migrate). In 28 species, all the birds migrate each year. In another 42 species, the northernmost birds go south for winter. By flying south in autumn, they avoid cold weather, short days, and less food. By going north in the spring, they can take advantage of longer days in which to hunt, and the abundant food supplies of the northern summer. Migrating can be dangerous: birds have to deal with bad weather and, much worse, people who shoot them. Hundreds of thousands of birds of prey are killed each year along migration routes; not for food, just for fun. Hunting, however, is not the worst of all the problems that raptors face. The greatest threats are habitat destruction and pollution. As the forests of the world are cut down, many raptors lose their homes, and die.

The Philippine eagle is one of the world's largest eagles, with a particularly massive beak

EAGLE IN DANGER
The Philippine eagle is the rarest eagle in the world. The forests that it lives in are disappearing fast. A captive breeding programme is trying to restore its numbers, but it is a very large eagle and needs large areas of undisturbed forest in which to hunt. Unless the forest is saved, this eagle will die out in the wild.

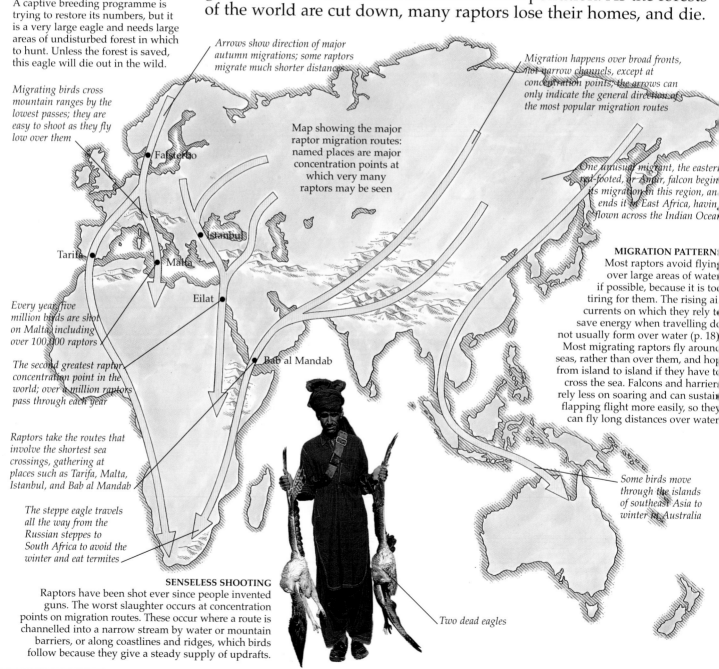

Arrows show direction of major autumn migrations; some raptors migrate much shorter distances

Migrating birds cross mountain ranges by the lowest passes; they are easy to shoot as they fly low over them

Map showing the major raptor migration routes: named places are major concentration points at which very many raptors may be seen

Migration happens over broad fronts, not narrow channels, except at concentration points; the arrows can only indicate the general direction of the most popular migration routes

One unusual migrant, the eastern red-footed, or Amur, falcon begins its migration in this region, and ends it in East Africa, having flown across the Indian Ocean

● Falsterbo

● Istanbul

Tarifa ●

● Malta

● Eilat

● Bab al Mandab

MIGRATION PATTERNS
Most raptors avoid flying over large areas of water if possible, because it is too tiring for them. The rising air currents on which they rely to save energy when travelling do not usually form over water (p. 18). Most migrating raptors fly around seas, rather than over them, and hop from island to island if they have to cross the sea. Falcons and harriers rely less on soaring and can sustain flapping flight more easily, so they can fly long distances over water.

Every year, five million birds are shot on Malta, including over 100,000 raptors

The second greatest raptor concentration point in the world; over a million raptors pass through each year

Raptors take the routes that involve the shortest sea crossings, gathering at places such as Tarifa, Malta, Istanbul, and Bab al Mandab

The steppe eagle travels all the way from the Russian steppes to South Africa to avoid the winter and eat termites

Some birds move through the islands of southeast Asia to winter in Australia

SENSELESS SHOOTING
Raptors have been shot ever since people invented guns. The worst slaughter occurs at concentration points on migration routes. These occur where a route is channelled into a narrow stream by water or mountain barriers, or along coastlines and ridges, which birds follow because they give a steady supply of updrafts.

Two dead eagles

Goshawks which live in the far north move south in harsh winters when prey becomes scarce

In flight, air pressure bends primary feathers upwards

MARATHON MIGRANTS
Steppe eagles travel from central Russia to South Africa each autumn. Another long-distance migrant is the eastern red-footed, or Amur, falcon. It travels from northern China to East Africa. Unusually, it flies over, not around, the Indian Ocean.

The steppe eagle migrates 13,000 km (8,000 miles) each autumn

SHOULD I STAY OR SHOULD I GO?
In some species, the birds will only move south in especially cold winters, or only move within their breeding range and not to an entirely different area, or only some of the birds in a region move. This is called "partial migration". A number of species, such as goshawks (above), sparrowhawks, and buzzards, are partial migrants. Often, adult birds can stay farther north than juveniles, because they are better at finding food.

American migrations tend to follow the lines of coasts and ridges, both of which provide plentiful updrafts to save raptors' energy

Cape May

The best place in the world to see raptors; over 2.5 million may pass through in one migration season

FROM SLAUGHTER TO SANCTUARY
Hawk Mountain in Pennsylvania, in the United States, is on the Kittatinny ridge, along which many raptors migrate. Once, many birds were shot as they flew over Hawk Mountain, but in 1934 it was bought by conservationists, who made it the world's first bird of prey sanctuary. They organized the world's first annual hawk count – since copied around the world – and led research into raptors.

The place and date of the ringing are written on the ring, so that the next scientists to trap the bird can trace its movements

Panama Canal

The birds using this route tend to follow the warmer coastline, rather than the colder mountains

A RING TO TRACK A RAPTOR WITH
It is hard to know when and where birds travel, and how far. One method scientists use to find out this information is to put little metal rings on birds' legs. Birds can be ringed in the nest when young, or trapped when older, ringed, and released. If they are trapped again elsewhere, or found dead, the information is sent to central collecting points. Some birds now wear transmitters tracked by satellites.

Only a few raptors migrate this far south

RAPTOR HOMES DEMOLISHED
The world's rain forests are being chopped down at a fast rate, destroying the homes and habitats of many raptors, and of many other living creatures, all irreplaceable. Habitat loss is the worst of all the problems affecting raptors, and a number of species, such as the Madagascar fish eagle, are close to extinction. Pollution is the second greatest problem, especially in countries where DDT and other long-lasting lethal pesticides are still in use.

Raptor records

THE FASTEST BIRD in the world, the bird with the greatest wing area, the bird that catches the largest quarry – all these are birds of prey. Fossil remains tell us of other remarkable raptors. The plains of Argentina hold the bones of a prehistoric condor-like bird that had a 25-ft (8-m) wingspan. In the recent past there was a species of eagle in New Zealand, Haast's eagle, that was one-third bigger than any living raptor. It became extinct only within the last thousand years. Many of today's most magnificent raptors may join it soon, thanks to human beings. They are in danger because of the damage we cause to the environment, damage which is increasingly rebounding on us. As one scientist said, "An environment unfit for raptors is an environment unfit for humanity."

SPEED KING
The gyrfalcon is the fastest of all the falcons in level flight. It may be the fastest in a stoop as well, because it is the largest and heaviest falcon. The high-speed tests done so far, however, have been on peregrines, so the highest recorded speeds are of peregrines.

LOFTIEST OF THEM ALL
Most birds do not fly high. They stay low, near their prey. Some, however, do go very high when migrating. The broad-winged hawk goes up to 16,500–20,000 ft (5,000–6,400 m). One Rüppell's griffon (above) hit a plane at 37,000 ft (10,000 m) above West Africa, but why this bird was flying so high is a mystery, as Rüppell's griffons do not migrate.

Falcons fold their wings further in than this when stooping really fast

WINGED LIGHTNING
When falcons stoop (dive) down on their prey, they travel faster than any other birds on earth. The peregrine falcon (left) is usually quoted as the fastest, but the other large falcons can probably stoop as fast. The maximum speed of a stoop is disputed. It is probably about 140 mph (225 km/h), although some estimates are higher.

LIVES ANYWHERE, EATS ANYTHING
The black kite is possibly the most common bird of prey in the world. A very adaptable Old World kite, it owes its success to its willingness to eat almost anything, from fish to the leftovers it finds in trash cans. In addition, it lives happily alongside humans. So do American and European kestrels, black vultures, and turkey vultures, also among the most populous raptors in the world.

A small but genuine raptor

PYGMY RAPTOR
The smallest birds of prey are the seven species of falconet, or pygmy falcon. Despite their size, they look just like the other birds of prey, on a smaller scale. They catch insects, lizards, and even birds nearly as big as themselves. The African pygmy falcon (above) is one of the smallest. The very smallest is the black-thighed falconet, which weighs 1–2 oz (28–56 g), and is 5.5–7 in (14–17 cm) high.

Black kites have the forked tails typical of kites

GIANT OF THE SKIES
The 10-ft (3-m) wingspan of the Andean condor is second in size only to that of the albatross. The condor's very broad wings give it the greatest wing area of any bird. It needs the wing area to lift it when it flies, because it can weigh up to 30 lb (13.5 kg). The condor is also probably the longest-lived of all the raptors: One condor was brought to the Moscow zoo as an adult (at least five years old) in 1892 and died there in 1964, when it must have been at least 77 years old. No bird in the wild would live anywhere near that long. Life expectancy generally increases with size among raptors, so condors probably do live the longest.

Labrador is included to show how big the condor's wings are

Imperial eagles have special protection, but they still may not survive

The white feathers on the back distinguish the imperial eagle from the much more common golden eagle

BACK FROM THE BRINK
At this moment in time, the California condor is probably the rarest bird of prey in the world. In the 1980s, shooting, habitat destruction, lead poisoning, and other causes brought the species to a point where there were only 27 birds left, and finally the last wild condors were brought into captivity for their own protection. Fortunately, they breed well in captivity, and the young are now being released into the wild.

California condors are famously ugly

A forest eagle, the harpy has relatively short, broad wings and a long tail

FATAL FEET
Harpy eagles are probably the most powerful of all raptors. They live in the rainforests of South America and hunt quarry as large as sloths and big monkeys. Female harpy eagles have talon-spans (from front to hind talon) of 8–9 in (20–23 cm). Their hind talons are up to 3.5 in (9 cm) long, bigger than the claws of a grizzly bear.

RAPTORS UNDER PRESSURE
A number of raptor species are endangered. One is the Spanish, or western, species of imperial eagle (above). The total population is probably down to 150 pairs. The causes of its decline include poisoning, a fall in the number of rabbits, and electrocution on power lines. A captive breeding program has been set up, but it has a long way to go. Around the world, habitat destruction is the greatest single problem facing birds of prey, especially for raptors on islands, where the original population is often very small and the birds have nowhere else to go.

The largest primary flight feathers in the world

Bird can withdraw its neck into ruff to keep warm

Andean condors have to run to get airborne on flat land; they prefer to jump off a cliff or run downhill

Index

Acknowledgments

Dorling Kindersley would like to thank:
Everyone at the National Birds of Prey Centre, near Newent, Gloucestershire, England (Craig Astbury, John Crooks, Monica Garner, Ian Gibbons, Debbie Grant, Breeze Hale, Angie Hill, Philip Jones, Kirsty Large, Mark Parker, Mark Rich, Jan Stringer).
The Booth Natural History Museum, Brighton (Jeremy Adams); Dr. Steve Parry.
Research and editorial assistance:
Sean Stancioff
Design assistance:
Julie Ferris, Iain Morris
Artwork: Bill Le Fever, Gilly

Newman, John Woodcock
Endpapers: Iain Morris
Index: Marion Dent
Additional photography:
Steve Gorton, Alex Wilson, C Laubscher
Picture credits
The publisher would like to thank the following for their kind permission to reproduce the images.
t=top, b=bottom, c=center, l=left, r=right
Ardea, London: Eric Dragesco 24tr.
British Museum: Front cover tl, Back cover tl, 50tr, 52tr/53tl.
Bruce Coleman Collection: Jane Burton 49bl, Raimund Cramm 38bl, Peter Davey 58tr, Francisco J. Erize

12bc, Pekka Helo 43tr, Gordon Langsbury 36tl, Mary Plage 27tl, Marie Read 44crb, N. Schwiatz 34cl, Uwe Walz 42br, Joseph Van Warmer 59tl, Staffan Widstrand 16br, Rod Williams 13tl.
Cornell Laboratory of Ornithology: L. Page Brown 38tl. **Dover Publications:** 10cra, 13cla, 32tl, 34c, 58tl. **Mary Evans Picture Library:** 40cl, 42tl, 43cl, 45tr, 46tr, 53br, 54tl.
Frank Lane Picture Agency: John Hawkins 39bc, E & D Hosking 56 bc, Alan Parker 47tr. **Giraudon, Paris:** 27cb, Avec Authorisation speciale de la Ville De Bayeux 52bl, 52tl.
Robert Harding Picture Library: Photri inc. 36cr. **Hawk Mountain Sanctuary Association, PA:** Wendy Scott 57cr. **Peter Newark's Pictures:**

42clb. **NHPA:** Martin Wendler 57br, Alan Williams 58cr.
Jemima Parry-Jones: 11tl, 38bc, 40tl, 45crb, 58br, Miguel Lopez 41tl. **Planet Earth:** D. Robert Franz 37tl, Nick Garbutt 47cla, William S. Paton 47tl, David A Ponton 10cl, Mike Read 49tr, Ronald S. Rogoff 43tc, Johnathan Scott 44tc, 44clb, Anup Shah 58cl.
Kati Poynor: 35tl.
RSPB: M. W. Richards 36bl.
Frank Spooner Pictures: Gamma/F. Soir 57bl.
Michael Zabé: 53tc.

Every effort has been made to trace the copyright holders. Dorling Kindersley apologizes for any unintentional omissions and would be pleased, in such cases, to add an acknowledgment in future editions.